SHAKING THE GLOBE

SHAKING THE GLOBE

Courageous Decision-Making in a Changing World

BLYTHE J. McGARVIE

WILEY

John Wiley & Sons, Inc.

Published by John Wiley & Sons, Inc., Hoboken, New Jersey.
Published simultaneously in Canada.

For general information on our other products and services or for technical support, please contact our Customer Care Department within the United States at (800) 762-2974, outside the United States at (317) 572-3993 or fax (317) 572-4002.

Wiley also publishes its books in a variety of electronic formats. Some content that appears in print may not be available in electronic books. For more information about Wiley products, visit our web site at www.wiley.com.

Library of Congress Cataloging-in-Publication Data:

McGarvie, Blythe J.
  Shaking the globe : courageous decision-making in a changing world / Blythe J. McGarvie.
    p. cm.
  Includes bibliographical references and index.
  ISBN 978-0-470-41157-5 (cloth)
  1. International trade.   2. International business enterprises.   3. International economic relations.   I. Title.
  HF1379.M43 2009
  658'.049—dc22   2008038663

Printed in the United States of America.

10 9 8 7 6 5 4 3 2 1

With gratitude to Mark, Brian, Cindy, and K. C. who shared my expatriate experience and continue to shake my quotidian and extraordinary life.

Contents

List of Figures

List of Tables

Foreword

Long before I entered the competitive business world of the National Football League, I was intrigued and excited by the opportunities of the global marketplace. In 1972, I founded International Forest Products, a manufacturer and trader of physical paper commodities. At the time, I believed that global economic expansion would be a natural by-product of improved global transportation infrastructure, the development of information technology, and the advancement in communications. International Forest Products is now the 40th largest exporter in the United States and the foundation on which The Kraft Group, my private holding company, was built.

Employing more than 5,000 people and doing business in more than 80 countries, serving tens of thousands of customers, The Kraft Group is comprised of businesses in paper distribution, paper and packaging manufacturing, sports and entertainment, real estate development, and private equity investment.

At The Kraft Group, we share Blythe McGarvie's passionate belief that global entrepreneurship without restrictions is the best recipe for true long-term economic success.

I know Blythe through our joint service on the board of directors of Viacom, where I have witnessed her passion for encouraging entrepreneurial business progress and her vision of how business can be a positive force for strengthening the global community. I share this vision with Blythe and am also troubled by those on both sides of the political spectrum who fear rather than embrace our rapidly changing global economy.

I have long believed that economic interdependence between countries is ultimately the only way to attain geopolitical stability on a macro scale. Blythe's work confirms this belief and explains away the fears of those who oppose global economic interdependence. In *Shaking the Globe*, she puts today's new globalization in historical and ideological context, presenting it as an opportunity for people everywhere to come closer together, improve their standards of living, and find fulfillment in personal initiative. Competition in the market, like on the gridiron, can bring out the best in all of us. Blythe encourages policy makers in business and politics not to avoid competition, but to use it for personal and societal change.

As a businessman and a concerned citizen, I have learned the importance of embracing change and diversity. What is new and different should be seen as exciting and the potential for growth. The leaders of this century will be those who welcome the challenge of what is new and turn it to their own, their company's, and their community's advantage. *Shaking the Globe* explains the basis for doing so, and in the process, serves as a guide for decision makers today and tomorrow.

ROBERT KRAFT
Chairman and Chief Executive Officer
The New England Patriots
August 2008

Prologue
The Globe Is Shaking

For the past 50 years, Americans and Western Europeans have been accustomed to setting the standards of business for the rest of the world. These standards include the practice of pushing Western cultural norms into other countries by imposing free enterprise capitalism, insisting on relatively equal rights for women, and exporting western tastes in food, music, and entertainment on the basis that they are superior to those found anywhere else. Now, Americans sense that a change in the world economy may allow other countries to shape the world's business standards and, in the process, impose a new set of cultural norms on international business. Rapid changes in the international community, including major restructurings in international business, are shaking the globe. Whether Westerners respond to this shaking as a trembling uncertainty or as an eruption of opportunity may determine how successfully they deal with the current changes.

Some Americans fear the new dynamics of the economy and believe U.S. economic development and employment will begin to decline. Rather than seeing the rise of the rest of the world as an opportunity, many Americans want to ignore the changes taking place or put up roadblocks to resist them. But, with the advent of a globally interconnected economy and the new financial realities it creates, change is not only inevitable—it is already in rapid motion. This book presents an argument for leaders of any business in developed or emerging markets to understand why and how the world is shaking so that they can move beyond current personal and institutional boundaries.

Many people find themselves caught off balance as the globe begins to shake faster and faster. But the answer is not to hunker down and erect defensive barriers—it is to take action. Our world needs leaders capable of collaborating with other cultures and taking prudent risks to create a new range of opportunities. The challenge of going global can be better understood once we understand how the following six considerations help Western business leaders adapt to the new global environment that is shaping the future:

1. Nonwestern cultural norms (particularly in China, India, and other emerging markets),
2. The technological and other skills of Generation Y,
3. Women as a labor resource,
4. The continuing role of shareholder interests,
5. The expanding role and changes to capitalism in creating entrepreneurs, and
6. The convergence of values stemming from the growth of democracy.

Many Americans fear that the global economy will cost them their jobs and purchasing power and that, in turn, it will force a reconsideration of American values. It is one thing to lose jobs to Indochina because employers located there can hire 14-year-old children and women cheaply, provide no health care, ignore safe workplace standards, hire and fire at will, and face no liability for environmental depredation. Yet, it is another thing to consider a twenty-first century America that must scale back its labor practices and deregulate to make America competitive once again. These fears are based on legitimate concerns but, I hope to lessen them, and the reactionary protectionist policies they engender, by demonstrating that global business changes offer opportunities to Americans.

Change is coming in large part because of the success of Western nations in convincing the rest of the world to embrace a market economy and democracy. This embracing of Western ideals by non-Western people has produced a greater degree of homogeneity in values and goals than the world has ever seen. I discuss this phenomenon of convergent and divergent values in Chapter 9 and argue that rather than fighting or worrying about cultural differences that arise on the margins of international business, leaders can begin to build relationships from a broad shared perspective.

I write from the perspective of my experiences in international business. My board work and professional experiences in India, China, Japan, France, Germany, the Netherlands, Finland, Chile, Mexico, the Philippines, Australia, Singapore, Indonesia, Turkey, Dubai, Russia, and beyond have helped shape my views that the world is shaking. In particular, I have learned the need to understand what it means to be a *global citizen*—to understand people and cultures different from my own in order to reach my goals and help others reach theirs. Business can provide a common language and common goals, but only when the parties' focus remains on business. In this book, I propose that Western business leaders must develop the courage to enter new cultures with a perspective of common interest—not as people holding an attitude of cultural or moral superiority or a self-image of being dominant. Some may see this as compromise, and I suppose it is. But it is also the only way to survive and profit as businesspeople in a global age. I argue that to make this compromise requires courage. This book offers a framework for identifying an individual's *courage quotient* and provides a foundation to understand those six considerations that will prepare business executives and their teams to take their organizations onto the global stage and succeed.

Why Go Global Now?

We stand on the shoulders of the giants who came before us. Four types of thinkers have influenced and motivated me to investigate and research the effect of business expanding beyond its domestic borders. The first and most consistent voice has been Peter Drucker, a professor and author of 39 books. His works are some of the most influential business books I have read. It has been my pleasure to meet and talk with this man who tested capitalism with the rigor of an academic and the empathy of a cross-cultural adventurer. He recognized that demographics explain much of the current and future business dynamics. I respect his lifelong discipline of digging deeply into a subject for several years and then later comparing his studies to find the connections between seemingly unconnected elements brought together in a multidisciplinary world. This practice taught me that, by evaluating the assumptions and methodology of various studies, I could better understand why and how business decisions were made.

The second major influence on this book were the people I met through my work on several boards of directors for companies as diverse as the leading global entertainment content company Viacom and Travelers Insurance, which is committed to the greater global community as well as the communities in which it does business. This board work alerted me to the present pace and demand for services and products around the world. We experienced new competition, accessed new sources of talent, found new channels for customers, and have had to use new suppliers in recent years. As the audit committee chairman for Accenture, for instance, I embarked on a trip to several cities in India to understand outsourcing, global strategies, customers, employees, and the risks and opportunities facing the firm. In 2005, the company employed about 3,000 employees based in India. By the time I returned for a visit to India in April 2008, Accenture had 37,000 employees based there out of its global workforce of 180,000 employees in 49 countries. That trip confirmed my beliefs that the multi-polar world was no longer theoretical; the changing dynamics between developed and emerging markets were happening before my eyes.

A third major influence on my research were the colleagues I met through a 12-month colloquy in which I participated, called

"Christian Faith and Economic Life." A group of 20 businesspeople, academics, and religiously trained professionals met on five occasions to discuss books and ideas in two-day sessions through a program organized by Professor Mark Valeri of Union Theological Seminary & Presbyterian School of Christian Education and Professor Doug Hicks of the University of Richmond, Jepson School of Leadership Studies. It was during that time that I first read and discussed the work of Laura Nash, a Senior Research Fellow at Harvard Business School. In *Just Enough: Tools for Creating Success in Your Work and Life* (cowritten with Howard Stevenson), the authors argue that the single greatest cause of today's frustration with what most of us call "success" is the failure to understand that real success requires skill in the art of complex decision making about noncomparable goals. The authors argue that you can measure success if you achieve your goals in the four distinct categories that represent conflicting human needs: happiness, achievement, significance, and legacy.

But Nash and Stevenson's research did not address the global ramifications and definitions of success. I needed to understand better the dynamics of business and how the interdependent world I observed affected the decision-making process. My own research revealed that different cultures and generations defined and measured success through different lenses. This led me to new discoveries on how cultural norms, the new workforce of today, and women's roles shape the decisions required to compete successfully and to offer products and services outside of the domestic marketplace. Some of this research led to my first book, *Fit In, Stand Out: Mastering the FISO Factor for Success in Business and Life* (New York, McGraw-Hill, 2006). While giving speeches and meeting people who wanted to learn from the system described in that book, I jotted down questions and started to see a pattern. In particular, the inquisitive, aspiring leaders in my audiences wanted to know more about how they could apply the leadership skills I discussed to expand the scope of their opportunities around the world. One of the messages in the book was that FISO leaders must embrace the idea of becoming global citizens. Yet, in our current business and political climate, I am shocked and disappointed by how many leaders retain an isolationist mindset—the idea that everything will be better if we only wall ourselves off from the rest of the world. This parochial and conventional thinking breeds fear and indecisiveness, hardly a recipe for future business or personal success. My passion is developing courageous business leaders and preventing isolationist thinking. This led me to create an assessment tool, the "Courage Quotient," which my company developed and statistically validated using results from hundreds of tests on a diverse group of businessmen and businesswomen. From this work, the assessment segments the response scores in four categories, including the Courageous quadrant. Courageous leaders understand that we live in a highly interdependent world, where 95 percent of the world's consumers live outside the United States and more than 200 million people live in countries other than the country of their birth. Global thinkers want to know how to convert this knowledge into action. This inspiration led to the suggestions presented in Part II of this book.

Finally, in writing this book, I must give homage to Thomas Friedman's book: *The World Is Flat: A Brief History of the Twenty-First Century* (New York: Farrar, Straus and Giroux, 2005). He explained to readers "the often bewildering global scene unfolding before their eyes . . . how the flattening of the world happened at the dawn of the twenty-first century; what it means to countries, companies, communities, and individuals; and how governments and societies can, and must, adapt." This survey of the changing world started a discussion about the new realities of the interconnected globe, but did not help explain how people can change their behavior to adapt to these realities. My work builds on recent trends and events shaking the globe and shows the forces you need to understand in order to make your own courageous business decisions.

The Journey Ahead

This book is not intended to be a comprehensive solutions manual for leaders as they undertake efforts to lead their organizations into the interconnected economy. The primary goal of this book is to improve decision making and identify what is required to develop the agility and ethics of global citizenship. Think of it as a guidebook for you to consult as you and your business engage in today's world. Courageous leaders understand that, before their followers can model new behaviors, they need first to transform themselves. Those managers who persist in thinking only about immediate concerns and gratification, keeping their blinders on to the future and the swirl of international activity, will soon find their careers at a standstill. Courageous leaders, on the other hand, understand that the best way to control their future is by gaining a better understanding of what going global means and how better to do business outside the United States.

Before we begin our journey around the shaking world, I offer some context in the book's first three chapters.

In Chapter 1, "Today's Interconnected Globe," I discuss the ways in which we are interconnected and how this interconnection presents opportunities for an individual who wants to expand his or her worldview. While Friedman's *The World Is Flat* develops a political point of view, this book reveals the world from the vantage point of business. I address the emergence of economies that represent the biggest shift in relative economic strength in the last hundred years. This is a key challenge for many individuals as companies expand their global reach. Chapter 1 discusses the rise of the multi-polar world.

Chapter 2, "Financial Realities," addresses the context of the globe's shifting financial order, in which investment opportunities are changing due to forces like the convergence of worldwide accounting standards, the varied mechanics of international markets, and the various degrees of transparency in different countries. Understanding these changes will separate globally savvy leaders from the also-rans who overlook the importance of the new bottom line.

Chapter 3, "The Four Types of Leaders," describes my research on both U.S. and non-U.S. individuals in many organizations. Leaders fall into one of four categories, each defined by a leader's degree of ability to embrace a leadership style that exudes both empathy and courage.

Part II of the book, "Connecting the World in Six Stops," discusses what forces will shake and shape our courage in the global economy.

In Chapter 4, "Cultural Norms," I further explore how people adjust to cultural norms. Different cultural norms may, at first, make us uncomfortable. However, the more we adapt to different norms, while maintaining our own value systems, the easier it will be for each of us to be successful. Beliefs, family, and time horizons are three major signposts of cultural norms. The key for global leaders is to understand how to change their action in consideration of these norms in different areas of the globe.

Today's young people will fill the jobs that will exist tomorrow around the world; and many of tomorrow's business leaders will not be Americans or Europeans. This is a demographic fact. That is why in Chapter 5, "Winning the Battle for Talent," I discuss how using new methods of communicating with youth to implement global business strategies is essential to the future prospects of any organization. In addition, leaders of all ages will need to hone their ability to harness the powers of multiple generations in today's workforce. Aligning personal and organization objectives will separate the winners from the laggards.

In Chapter 6, "Women Working," I attempt to rebut the fears of many women that globalization is counterproductive to women's rights and argue that in the new economy it will be necessary to find ways to keep women in the workforce. Across the globe, women have not achieved the same management or educational levels as men. It may be that cultural norms or laws have prevented women from entering the workforce or progressing to executive levels. The international community and many business organizations recognize that the talents possessed by 50 percent of the world's population is currently being wasted. Enlightened leaders may tap into this underutilized talent by educating, hiring, and retaining women in business at all levels of the enterprise—from entry level to board positions.

Shareholders do not invest money for philanthropic reasons. That's why in Chapter 7, "Shareholder Interests," I discuss how shareholders today come from many different countries and organizations with motives different from those held by the founder of a company. Sovereign wealth funds (SWF) demand a long-term return on their equity. Institutional funds, on the other hand, demand a shorter to medium-term outlook. Knowing who invested capital in your organization will help you navigate these uncharted waters. Sometimes funds can be used for purposes other than reinvesting in the business. Knowing who and what type of investor you have will change how you can compete globally and what types of returns and reinvestment opportunities your company must strive to provide.

In Chapter 8, "Entrepreneurs from A to Z," I assert that entrepreneurial spirit is essential for success in today's world. Capitalism promotes the free flow of capital and labor which breeds innovation and improves the standard of living around the interconnected globe. In this chapter, I discuss how leading global companies are disaggregating their operations around the globe to take advantage of the best talent and competitive economies to spur their own continued growth. I also alert the reader to tools being used to identify where the best opportunities exist today and in the future.

Individuals have their own moral values, which must be understood in the global context. In Chapter 9, "Values and Global Context," I present a cultural value framework to navigate through free markets that are emerging in non-Western cultures. How you communicate and work in a culture foreign to you will depend on your perception and understanding of how the individuals' values are rooted in their home country. Understanding how to leverage and work in new cultures, while not giving up your own belief system, will separate the mountain climbers who make it to the summit from those who are stuck at base camp—or from those who plunge to their demise.

In the Epilogue, I provide some suggestions for you to use to continue updating your mastery of going global. Globalization is happening with or without you. To be a leader, you must learn how to take advantage of the opportunity globalization presents by:

- Understanding how you can transcend existing biases and prepare for the new world to keep your business growing.
- Embracing strategies to develop transformational global leadership skills to establish beachheads for future growth opportunities.
- Learning how to stimulate coordination and cooperation across national borders to create a lasting and rewarding relationship with people with whom you will be connected.

It is time to learn how to shift from thinking that everything you know about the world of business is being shaken to where you and your organization are doing the shaking.

PART

Preparing for an Adventure

CHAPTER 1

Today's Interconnected Globe

Consider a world in which China accounts for more than a third of the world's industrial output.[1] Meanwhile, India and the major European economies make up another 33 percent. The United States, on the other hand, contributes a mere 2 percent of the global gross domestic product (GDP). Does this sound like a horror story of things to come? Perhaps. But these figures, according to research published by economist Martin Wolf, actually depict the global economy in 1820. Before the Industrial Revolution, Western economies waited for sailing fleets and horse-drawn wagons to deliver riches like silk and spices from the Far East. Worldwide economies, of course, are nothing new; they have functioned for hundreds of years with political and economic empires dictating their terms. Over the past 150 years, the world's economic power has been concentrated in the hands of Americans, Europeans, and the Japanese. We are now, however, entering another growth period for non-U.S. economies. Today, 95 percent of the world's consumers, constituting two-thirds of its purchasing power, reside outside the United States. By 2015, the list of the world's top 10 economies, which already includes cities in China, will grow to encompass other emerging economies such as cities in India and South Korea.[2] The twenty-first century, therefore, will no longer be an age of empires or even one of the lone economic superpowers. We are instead witnessing a new era of economic interconnectedness. As Parag Khanna wrote in his piece for the *New York Times*, "Waving Goodbye to Hegemony":

> *The more we appreciate the differences among American, European, and Chinese worldviews, the more we will see the planetary stakes of the new global game. Previous eras of balance of power have been among European powers sharing a common culture. The Cold War, too, was not truly an "East-West" struggle; it remained essentially a contest over Europe. What we have today, for the first time in history [sic], is a global, multicivilizational, multipolar battle.*[3]

Back to the Future

Accenture, a global consulting company, describes this new global economic model in which the uni-polar dominance of nations like the United States has ended as the *rise of the multi-polar world*. Numerous developing economies now enjoy the economic power and influence formerly held exclusively by empires. These developing regions or countries contribute an ever-growing share of the world's output, trade, and investment. Accenture's 2008 report, "The Rise of the Multi-Polar World," indicates that developing nations now account for some 49 percent of global GDP—and should, within two decades, surpass the combined GDP of what we now call the "developed world."[4] The report's authors assert: "Globalization is now becoming a two-way process in which developing/emerging economies are changing from passive recipients to active shapers of globalization."

Tremendous change frequently provokes resentment and reactionary defensiveness. Executives and managers who allow such

Table 1.1 Top 15 Consumer Markets in 2025

Country	2005*	2025*	Growth Rate (%)
China	3,088	14,527	8.0
United States	7,335	12,512	2.7
India	1,924	4,264	4.1
Russia	749	2,489	6.2
Japan	1,780	2,291	1.3
United Kingdom	1,058	1,707	2.4
Germany	1,180	1,512	1.2
Brazil	757	1,465	3.4
France	917	1,374	2.0
Italy	836	1,168	1.7
Mexico	648	1,139	2.9
Canada	539	1,045	3.4
Spain	560	945	2.7
South Korea	413	914	4.1
Australia	339	592	2.8
World	*30,374*	*54,998*	*3.0*

*Based on consumer spending in billions of U.S. dollars.
Source: Accenture, "The Rise of the Multi-Polar World," 2007, p. 22.

attitudes to influence policies deserve the fate that awaits them. Americans, in particular, have grown accustomed to a world in which they have great economic, cultural, and political influence. Many still perceive globalization and outsourcing as threats to their well-being. The news media play to these fears by focusing on horror stories of towns and cities decimated by factory closures due to foreign competition. A poll conducted by the *New York Times* and CBS News in the spring of 2008 found that 68 percent of Americans favor tighter restrictions on free trade in an effort to head off threats like China's deep pool of cheap labor—the highest percentage since the poll was begun in the 1980s and a substantial increase over the same poll taken in 2000, which concluded that 56 percent favored tighter restrictions on trade.[5]

However, competition from abroad benefits Americans as much as it hurts them. A company such as Wal-Mart, which is so often criticized for using its size and buying power to lower its costs, established a new standard for low-cost production by sourcing outside of the United States. If Americans want to buy products at cheap prices, they must endure having these products manufactured by cheap labor. The lower cost of labor gained by outsourcing creates new standards for costs as well as improved efficiencies. Wal-Mart, however, is only one marketplace. During 2007, as the U.S. dollar weakened, competition for U.S. real estate and services brought money into the United States, benefiting U.S. landowners, businesses, and investors. As the global economy continues to change, Americans, as producers, sellers, and buyers must change with it.

India prepares more than 400,000 U.S. tax returns every year and China produces the bulk of children's toys sold in the United States, indicating that geography no longer controls how tasks are assigned in both the service and manufacturing sector economies. Lower cost drives these task assignments.[6] Yet, some leaders of both companies and governments respond to new cost standards by ignoring them or by hoping that the situation will simply return to what it once was. Media figures Pat Buchanan[7] and Lou Dobbs[8] use their public platforms to sound the alarm and take up defensive positions. They imply that our lives will improve if we wall ourselves off from the new economy. But this approach does not protect us from or fend off competition. In fact, it cripples our ability to respond with vigor. As William D. Green, the chairman and CEO of Accenture, put it in his firm's report: "We are at a critical moment as a global economy. Move one way, toward greater freedom of trade, the possibilities of new technologies, the promotion of education and skills training on a vast scale, and the opportunities are endless. Step the other way, toward the retrenchment into tariffs, a rejection of the newest new things and a reluctance to change the social and cultural patterns of generations, and those opportunities could be lost."[9]

Bringing Down the Walls

Mr. Gorbachev, tear down this wall!

—Ronald Reagan, June 12, 1987[10]

Many Americans refer to 9/11 as a critical date in their nation's history; Europeans also consider 9/11 a critical day—but for different reasons. November 9, 1989, written as 9/11/1989 in the common European calendar format, is the day the Berlin Wall came down. It is one of the most important days not only in recent European history, but for the global economy as well. The fall of that wall opened up new opportunities for collaboration among nations.

Europe's recent embrace of a multicultural and cooperative economic system presents a model for Americans to consider. In 1993, European nations formed the European Union (EU) as an unprecedented effort at collaborative free trade that today boasts 27 member nations.[11] In 2007, the collective GDP of the EU nations was $16.6 trillion, representing about 30 percent of the global GDP. To form this unified EU, European leaders overcame popular opposition to the loss of local currencies, fear of new work patterns, and even the subordination of national economic control to an umbrella agency based in Brussels. It wasn't easy for the French to give up the franc, for instance, or for the Italians to trade in the lira for the euro. However, the EU has been an undisputed economic success. Not surprisingly, African nations are now discussing a future African Union, and China is leading the way toward a new East Asian Community.[12] Cooperation between countries in close proximity provides an initial cross-cultural experience. In each of these instances, national currencies, values, laws, and many other cultural expressions must be transformed to serve regional rather than parochial needs. New economic rules are being formed without the participation of the United States.

Americans, in turn, may have to face the loss of cultural and financial controls similar to those experienced by Europeans in the past decade in order to maintain their lifestyles and their economic and political stability. Europe has learned its lesson. As Jose Manuel Barroso, the European Commission president said: "The right approach to shape and respond to globalization is to build an integrated and open Europe, socially and economically dynamic—and highly competitive."[13]

The North American Free Trade Agreement (NAFTA) is a very small and hesitant step in the right direction for the United States. Yet, even it has spurred political outrage and cultural defensiveness. The new model of global interconnectedness, like that embraced by Barroso and others, is one U.S. leaders ignore at their peril. "Borders don't protect us," Jim Steinberg, vice president and director of the foreign policy studies program at the Brookings Institution, said. "The movement of people, ideas, capital, and goods has now become a fact of life."[14]

The Interconnected Globe Hits Home

I first became aware of the global economy in 1969 when I was 12 years old. As an assignment for school, I wrote about the impact of the Prague Spring, that moment in history when the Russian military invaded Czechoslovakia to clamp down on the democratic reforms begun by Alexander Dubcek in January 1968. (The country would remain occupied for another decade.) The Russians raised barriers to further separate the East from the West. My blithe conclusion in my paper was that we would have trouble obtaining "the wonderful hops to make our beer." One month later, I changed schools and, during that quarter, a boy named Jiri Sonek joined the class. The thing I noticed first about him was that he wore the same two shirts over and over. I later learned that he and his family had fled their home city of Prague during the invasion with literally one suitcase to hold all of their belongings. Of course, I didn't really appreciate what it meant to Jiri and his family to emigrate from Czechoslovakia to the United States to escape oppression, even though I had written a paper about their home country. In time, I remember realizing how narrow-minded my first response was to such an historic event. Why did I worry about hops for beer? Why did I focus on what a refugee was wearing rather than asking him what he had escaped from? To his credit, Jiri took full advantage of the new opportunities his parents had given him. Today, he is Dr. Sonek, a medical director of maternal fetal medicine at a hospital in Dayton, Ohio. When I think of Jiri today, a man who had to reinvent himself to survive, I realize these encounters broadened my worldview and perspective about the interconnected world.

One informative source leaders can use for help in understanding the shifts in the balance of globally competitive markets is the World Economic Forum (WEF). The WEF is an independent, not-for-profit international organization based in Geneva, Switzerland, that is committed to improving the state of the world by engaging leaders in partnerships to shape global, regional, and industrial agendas. One of the groups associated with WEF is the Global Competitiveness Network (GCN), a team that works with leading academics worldwide to tap into the latest thinking and research on global competitiveness. Beginning in 1979, the GCN has produced an annual study called *The Global Competitiveness Report* that is considered by governments, academics, and business leaders to be the most comprehensive and authoritative assessment of the comparative strengths and weaknesses of national economies.[15] The rankings are calculated from both publicly available data and the *Executive Opinion Survey*, a comprehensive annual survey conducted by the WEF together with its network of leading research institutes and business organizations (partner institutes) in the countries covered by the report. For its 2007 report, more than 11,000 business leaders were polled in 131 countries.

The report ranks the 131 nations from A to Z—Albania to Zimbabwe—and computes a global competitive index for each country based on the relative competitiveness of its economy. To do this, each country is rated in 12 categories, called pillars, which include: *Institutions, Infrastructure, Macroeconomic Stability, Health and*

Primary Education, Higher Education and Training, Goods Market Efficiency, Labor Market Efficiency, Financial Market Sophistication, Technological Readiness, Market Size, Business Sophistication, and *Innovation*. Each pillar is then divided into specific components, for instance the *Innovation* pillar includes "company spending on R&D" and "capacity for innovation." To arrive at the overall rankings, experts were asked to assign a value from 1 (does not meet the needs of the global economy) to 7 (meets the needs of the global economy) to each of the 110 components that comprise the 12 pillars. The higher the rating a country received for the 12 pillars, the higher competitive ranking it received. Along with the ranking, the report also listed the most problematic factors or biggest threats to the future competitive prospects of each economy. In other words, the WEF's index is not only extremely useful in pinpointing the most competitive economies of today—but it also indicates those economies that will soon find themselves under siege along with those that are well-positioned to grow rapidly.

Looking at the results from the 2007 WEF report, we find that while the U.S. economy is ranked first in overall competitiveness, earned largely on the strength of the U.S. consumer market and its strong tradition of innovation; the top three most problematic factors in doing business in the United States are tax rates, tax regulations, and an inefficient bureaucracy. In the opinion of the experts asked by the WEF, these are the biggest factors that threaten the future competitiveness of the U.S. economy. In fact, the United States ranks only seventy-fifth in the world when it comes to macroeconomic stability because the country faces serious threats from its low national savings rate and the enormous debts and trade deficits created by U.S. government spending.

When you look deeper at the rankings, you see that the education systems in the United States cannot keep up with the new demands of the global economy, nor can it keep fueling the types of innovative breakthroughs in technology that have been the economy's strength over the past 50 years. Not only do the WEF experts rank the work ethic of American workers as low when compared to many countries, but they also raise a warning flag about how inadequately educated Americans are given the needs of the inter-connected economy. In an era where computer and engineering skills are valued at a premium, the United States ranks forty-fifth when it comes to the quality of math and science education provided to its young people. This means that U.S. companies will have no choice but to look beyond their national borders to find the nec-essary human capital they will need to remain competitive in the high-tech, high-growth sectors of the future.

Simply stated, by analyzing the information supplied by the WEF and similar organizations, today's leaders can stop knee-jerk responses to news supplied by the subjective news media and instead begin understanding the news in context of the future trends. This will improve decision making and will increase the likelihood of discovering new opportunities before they emerge elsewhere.

Jingoism, however, can be a particularly daunting barrier for leaders in the interconnected economy. Americans in particular suc-cumb to the sometimes virulent habit of waving the national flag as a means of protesting change. "Made in America" has become a ral-lying cry not only for things like Ford and Chevy trucks sold in the heartland, but also for opponents of everything from outsourcing to immigration. Politicians and commentators place the blame for economic malaise and downturn on the companies who send jobs overseas. Pat Buchanan even goes so far as to say America is coming apart as a direct result of its multiethnic diversity.

The American economy and others will flounder without a pipeline of diverse talent. Studies published by the National Foun-dation for American Policy decisively concluded that increasing the number of H-1B visas granted to foreign professionals would not only help spur growth in U.S.-based companies, it would also create more jobs for Americans.[16] An H-1B visa is a nonimmigrant visa that allows U.S. companies to employ foreign guest workers in occupa-tions only when qualified U.S. citizens or residents are not available. And yet Congress, under pressure from constituents who operate on fear rather than on facts, continues to use an arbitrary number to decide how many foreign workers will be allowed into the country each year. (The limit was set at 65,000 visas for 2008.) As Microsoft Chairman Bill Gates said in his testimony before Congress, "We live in an economy that depends on the ability of innovative companies to attract and retain the very best talent, regardless of nationality or citizenship." Due to better educational systems and more demanding cultural norms, young people in other countries provide much of that "best talent."

Americans don't have a monopoly on xenophobia. Japanese restaurants in Tokyo protest the number of stars given to them by the distinctly French Michelin Guide[17] or Russian hockey players eschew the greater salaries available in the North American-based National Hockey League to play at home.[18] Cultural differences remain barriers to a truly connected global market. As Parag Khanna writes in the *New York Times*:

> The rise of China in the East and of the European Union within the West has fundamentally altered a globe that recently appeared to have only an American gravity—pro or anti. As Europe's and China's spirits rise with every move into new domains of influence, America's spirit is weakened. The E.U. may uphold the principles of the United Nations that America once dominated, but how much longer will it do so as its own social standards rise far above this lowest common denominator? And why should China or other Asian countries become "responsible stakeholders," in former Deputy Secretary of State Robert Zoellick's words, in an American-led international order when they had no seat at the table when the rules were drafted? Even as America stumbles back toward multilateralism, others are walking away from the American game and playing by their own rules.[19]

In our highly interdependent world, we cannot ignore non-U.S. cultures and the demographic and social forces they bring to bear—nor can leaders of other nations overlook the opportunities that exist outside of their turf. Stopping the world and getting off has never been an option. Neither can we go back to the way things were. Rather, we need to reach out and embrace change, shaping it to our benefit. Fueled by technology like the Internet, satellite communications, and fast computer processors, we now have almost instant access to far-flung populations and cultures that represent tremendous avenues for growth, not threats. Indeed, the best way to mitigate future economic risks is to invest in emerging markets. The fact that U.S. ownership in foreign equities has increased more than 14 percent over the past few years indicates that our future-looking leaders already understand we are at a historical inflection point that requires them to avoid conventional paths and avoid retreating behind walls.[20] We need our leaders to adapt to and participate in many new and different cultures not only to tap new sources of talent, but also to open new markets for their companies' goods or services. We need to cultivate leaders who are hungry to learn the facts about key existing connections and decide how they will affect not only their lives, but those of the people they work alongside of as well. That also means having leaders willing to immerse themselves in the global economy by traveling to cultures different from their own, and then embracing them rather than forming second-hand opinions parroting what they hear from media personalities. As Joel Kurtzman, a senior fellow at the Milken Institute and co-author of *Global Edge*, writes: "In the United States in particular, international news reports are often better at misinforming than they are at educating business leaders."[21] After all, the difference between a leader and a follower is the courage to take on the responsibility of making change. Fortunately, there are already such leaders out there not shaking from fear, but bent on shaking loose new opportunities.

Five Factors That Shake the Multi-Polar World

Mark Foster, the group chief executive of Accenture's management consulting and integrated markets practice, had great insight as to what will drive high performance of both businesses and governments in the multi-polar world. This knowledge can help shape the characteristics needed by leaders to confront the new conditions. Mark thinks the companies and governments that master the following five factors will be the winners in the new wave of competition that will shake the interconnected world in which we live:[22]

1. *Developing talent:* By the year 2050, 97 percent of the 438 million people that make up the global labor force will come from developing economies. As the populations in most Western economies age and, in some cases, even shrink, competition for talent will intensify. It's a race in which countries with tight immigration laws such as the United States could find themselves quickly falling behind. Looking ahead to the workforce of 2020, 70 percent are already out of both high school and college, so businesses will need to train and retrain talent.

2. *Attracting multidirectional capital flows:* In the past, companies based in developed nations looked to emerging markets for expansion opportunities. This practice, known as *foreign direct investment,* has since been turned on its head. Emerging economies now account for 17 percent of global direct investment. As there is for talent, there is growing competition around the world to access this new source of capital.

3. *Participating in new consumer markets:* Emerging markets are no longer seen merely as low-cost suppliers of goods and services—they have now become crucial destination markets in their own right. Consumers in countries such as China, India, and Mexico are expected to account for more than half of global consumption by 2025. (See Table 1.1 for a breakdown of the Top 15 Consumer Markets in 2025.) Accessing these markets will be key to the growth of any transnational company or rival emerging economy.

4. *Winning the battle for resources:* Led by economies such as China, emerging economies have spurred an 85 percent increase in world energy consumption since 2000. This increase in demand for energy is mirrored by a surge in demand for commodities such as wheat and copper. The demand for energy and raw materials is expected to increase further in the coming years, which means that competition will also increase for these scarce resources.

5. *Reading the new map of innovation:* As the number of engineers produced in the United States continues to drop, and tighter immigration laws keep prospective international students away, new clusters of technology have emerged in up-and-coming innovation hotbeds like Beijing, Bengalooru, Greater Seoul, and Krakow. China, for example, holds 12 percent of the world's patents for nanotechnology. In short, emerging economies continue to move up the innovation food chain, evolving from technological imitators to epicenters for R&D breakthroughs.

Leaders who are already adapting to the realities of our interconnected world show the tremendous success available to those who look forward instead of backward. Consider, for example, the actions of a division management team of General Electric (GE).[23] Founded in 1890, you might expect GE to advertise its heritage and longevity whenever it could. However, as a company built on manufacturing, GE, which has its headquarters in Fairfield, Connecticut, is struggling to compete and keep its foothold in the U.S. market. The company's revenues continue to grow, largely due to the strength of its sales overseas. In 2007, for the first time in the company's history, sales from outside the United States outstripped domestic accounts. One source of this growth is attributable to a division of GE based in Erie, Pennsylvania, that produces 150-ton railroad locomotives that typically carry a price tag of $4 million apiece. Facing a dwindling market for its locomotives in the United States, the future of this division looked dismal. Like many towns founded on heavy industries, the town of Erie faced the prospect of losing more jobs if this particular GE division failed. Fortunately, for both GE and Erie, they had a secret weapon: John Dineen, president of the division. Rather than shutter the 100-year-old locomotive plant, Dineen pushed internal efforts to improve quality and cut waste while he searched the global marketplace to find new customers in rapidly developing economies such as Brazil, Kazakhstan, and China, where trains remain an integral component of the transportation structure. China alone bought 200 trains in 2007, which leads Dineen to joke that Erie is now one of the few areas in the United States to have a trade surplus with an emerging superpower. "What we are doing in Erie is really a play on globalization," he says. Rather than waving the flag and blaming others for his division's struggles, he looked for new opportunities for growth. Today, Dineen's division, with $4.5 billion in revenues for 2007, is twice as big as it was five years ago. GE has emerged as the world leader in producing diesel-electric freight locomotives: a clear success story from the multi-polar world.

GE is not alone in cultivating leaders who see opportunities instead of threats in the international market. Caterpillar Inc., for example, is another heavy industry company that has hitched its future growth to selling its backhoe loaders, harvesters, hydraulic excavators, and paving equipment overseas. Like GE's locomotive division, more than half of Caterpillar's $45 billion in annual revenue now comes from countries such as China, Russia, India, and rapidly industrializing countries in the Middle East. In fact, demand for its products is now at a level that warrants the planning of new plants in China and India to supply its customers. "No matter what happens, we're going to flex our workforce, flex our manufacturing facilities to meet the demand of our customers wherever they are," David Burritt, the company's CFO, has said.[24] Large, public corporations are not alone in seizing opportunities beyond traditional borders. Entrepreneurs who shake the globe seek currency advantages in attracting international customers and investors to their home country.

We are, as these examples help illustrate, witnessing the resurgence of the "transnational company," a term used by business guru Peter Drucker to describe a company for whom national boundaries have become irrelevant. A transnational company is distinct from its multinational cousin because its leaders look upon the world—not just individual nations—as its market. As Drucker put it in 1997, "The transnational company is not totally beyond the control of national governments. It must adapt to them. But these adaptations are exceptions to policies and practices decided on for worldwide markets and technologies. Successful transnational companies see themselves as separate, nonnational entities. This self-perception is evidenced by something unthinkable a few years ago: A transnational top management."[25]

Drucker possessed an uncanny ability to see into the future. But other leaders in the world today provide additional case studies from which we can learn. For example, Bruno Bich, son of the founder of Société Bic Group, under whom I served as executive vice president and chief financial officer from 1999 to 2002, understands the notion of what a transnational leader is. Bic recruited me to its Paris headquarters from Portland, Maine—part of its strategy to tap into new talent worldwide. Bruno once told me that you can't be successful relying entirely on your own people—you need to enroll others. In other words, in an interconnected world, we need to collaborate with people who may be foreign to us and learn from them. What's interesting is how Bic, the company, has itself become transnational by blending in and blurring traditional boundaries in what some have called combining a global scope with a local focus. Many Americans, for example, think of Bic as a made-in-the-United-States kind of company, when it is truly a French company. The same principle holds for Bic subsidiaries in South Africa or the United Kingdom; many countries perceive Bic as a local company. Bic recruits and trains employees from all over the world to think like transnational leaders, hiring local leaders when possible—all of which has contributed to Bic's growth and continued success over the years. Rather than think of the multi-polar world as some kind of barrier or hurdle to overcome, therefore, Bic is one example of a transnational company that, because of its exceptional leaders, has transformed itself to take advantage of new global opportunities. As Robert Louis Stevenson wrote, "There are no foreign lands. It is the traveler only who is foreign."

What, then, are some of the keys to grooming transnational leaders? One key is that today's leaders need to have the courage to move beyond the comfort zone in their home country and venture out into the world to both learn and embrace new cultures. As Tom Neff, U.S. chairman of Spencer Stuart, has said: "The value is clear: for CEOs, an experience overseas can provide a real competitive edge."[26]

Key Points to Consider

- In our interconnected global economy, it takes courage to look beyond cultural barriers and create new customs for the future. How do you keep past products and traditions and modify them to be relevant for future business?

- A key success factor for leading in the interconnected economy is responding quickly to the five factors of the multi-polar world. Every country and culture works differently. How can the successful leader search for business outside his domestic market and accelerate his decision-making pace?

- Successful leadership requires flexibility. Do you make a plan and alter it regularly to reflect updated financial results or current conditions?

- With change comes volatility. What steps can you take to look beyond the fears of others to see the opportunities that lie ahead?

- To fit in and stand out in the interconnected economy is to recognize that success comes from collaboration. Have you identified the champions for going global who can help you?

In short, the new realities of the global markets mean that we need leaders with the courage to break from the old and begin again with the new. The next chapter explores how new financial realities increase the urgency for consistently reporting results and how it reflects market volatilities.

CHAPTER

2

Financial Realities

Given my background in accounting and finance, it is not surprising that I have been particularly attuned to the key financial drivers that, in my opinion, many business leaders have yet to grasp fully. When these leaders attempt to confront our changing economic landscape, they face a test for which they aren't prepared. Although the language of business is finance, many leaders have not learned the nuances of this language and struggle to use a framework to identify and evaluate those companies that know how to compete successfully in global free markets. In this chapter, we explore the factors driving the new financial realities of the interconnected globe.

Realities of Supply and Demand

The first thing we learn in a basic economics class is to draw supply and demand curves. These curves serve as the basis for the primary law of market theory, namely that if demand exceeds supply, prices will increase; if demand dips below supply, prices will fall. This model becomes more complex when you begin to add in external factors like taxes, inflation, or interest rates, but the basic premise holds true whether you are talking about theoretical widgets or the price of an ounce of gold. When we apply this model to the interconnected globe, we find that whereas just a few decades ago a handful of countries vied for the supply of everything from oil to wheat, which kept demand levels fairly predictable, we now are witnessing a dramatic spike in the demand for commodities. One-time suppliers are now purchasers. For example, India, the world's second-largest rice exporter in 2007, began imposing restrictions on overseas sales in March 2008 in order to meet domestic demand for the product. India, recognizing that its domestic buyers lacked the purchasing power of foreign consumers, began banning exports of nonbasmati rice, one of a series of protectionist measures. In addition, hypergrowth in emerging countries has led to surges of purchases ranging from China importing steel and concrete, India buying industrial metal, and Middle Eastern countries buying food at unprecedented levels.[1] That demand spike is, in fact, rapidly outstripping the ability of the market to deliver a steady supply of those commodities. The direct result is that prices are rising throughout the world, as shown in Figure 2.1.

Perhaps no commodity creates the direct and indirect price spikes based on its availability and price as much as oil. Not so long ago it was thought that the supply of oil would probably last through the twenty-first century and beyond. In 1999, for instance, the *Economist* magazine reported that the price of oil, at $10 a barrel, was artificially high and that, given the prevailing trends and expanded production on the part of the OPEC nations, the price would drop to about $5 a barrel.[2] Wrong. Prices went above $147 a barrel recently and, have as of this printing, declined to $114. Prices rise partially due to the population growth—and a corresponding increase in demand for cars, trucks, and airplanes in emerging markets. Some worry that there may not be enough oil to meet the next generation's demands. Because of higher drilling costs and political barriers, worldwide oil production remains relatively flat, despite what increasingly promises to be an acute shortage.[3] William Chandler, an energy expert with the Carnegie Endowment for International

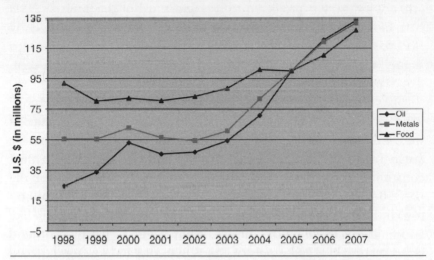

Figure 2.1　Index of Commodity Prices *Data source:* International Monetary Fund, base year 2005, www.imf.org/external/data.htm.

Peace, estimates that by 2030, India and China will import as much oil as the United States and Japan combined do today. According to the official energy statistics of the Energy Information Administration, the U.S. imports about 20 million barrels per day; China is forecasted to increase their current imports from 7.5 million to 16 million barrels in 2030. India imports 2.7 million barrels today, with varying forecasts for its future consumption predicting that it could be as large as China's demand. Such a level of demand would mean that to supply just India and China at least five times as much oil as Saudi Arabia produces today would be necessary. Leaders need to address the new realities created by these changes—realities that are often far more complex than they seem on the surface.

Consumers feel the impact of high fuel prices when they fill their gas tanks. The spiraling cost of a gallon of gas spurs interest in fuel-saving technologies such as hydrogen- or hybrid-powered cars and the development of alternative fuels such as bio-fuels.[4] Ethanol, which is made from corn, has drawn particular interest from farmers who have long suffered from flat prices for their crops. In fact, the ethanol industry is projected to use one-third of the autumn 2008 corn harvest, an allotment twice the level used for ethanol as recently as 2005.[5] Farmers benefit further because when they sell their crops as fuel, the supply of food is reduced in the market, which, in turn, drives up food prices.

As emerging markets become more established and their populations become more affluent, their lifestyles begin to change as well. Following in the path of Western consumers, many Chinese are increasingly substituting meat for rice in their diets.[6] World meat consumption has more than doubled on a per capita basis over the past 50 years, with total meat consumption rising from 71 million tons in 1961 to 284 million tons in 2007. While that might seem like an innocuous trend on the surface, it has begun to have a profound effect on the price and supply of grains like corn and soy, used to feed cattle worldwide. The grains that used to feed people are now used to fatten animals. But it takes about two to five times more grain to produce the same amount of calories raising livestock for meat than if humans consumed grain directly, according to Rosamond Naylor, an associate professor of economics at Stanford University. These factors have, at least in part, led to what U.N. Secretary-General Ban Ki-moon now calls "a global food crisis."[7] This crisis is likely to have an indirect impact on the supply and prices charged for products in developed nations. Discount bulk grocers, like Costco and Sam's Club, have already placed purchase limits on the amounts of certain raw grains their customers can buy per shopping visit.

A major indirect effect resulting from supply and demand shifts has been the greater focus on the environment. Globally minded citizens are rightfully worried about global warming and fear that additional automobiles and planes will increase air pollution. So too will the changes in food consumption. According to the U.N.'s Food and Agriculture Organization, some 30 percent of the earth's arable land is used to support livestock production, which some scientists argue produces more greenhouse gases than all of the world's transportation systems put together.[8] American retailers, whose customers can afford marginal cost increases to ensure a healthier future, are assuming a disproportionate burden in addressing these concerns.

Wal-Mart, for instance, has already begun to push its suppliers in China—where Wal-Mart accounts for about 30 percent of all foreign purchases—to adopt environmentally sustainable practices.[9] Individuals who understand the rules of supply and demand and apply them to the conditions in the interconnected global market will sell into new markets, find sourcing opportunities, and change how they do business. But these rules also mean that leaders need to think about the ripple effect their decisions can have around the world.

The Color of Money

The credit crunch that evolved from the collapse of the subprime mortgage market in the United States in 2007 provides an excellent example of the role of supply and demand in a global economy. As banks lost liquidity on their balance sheets by building required statutory reserves and raising their standards to determine credit-worthy borrowers, they stopped lending money, particularly to anyone with investments connected to the real estate market. While investment banks like Bear Stearns encountered trouble because their supply of credit evaporated, the effects from that cash drought rippled far and wide through the interconnected economy. The island nation of Iceland has been hit hard by the credit crunch (as part of the fallout of the U.S. mortgage debacle) because it relied quite heavily on accessing outside capital to fuel its economy.[10] Now that U.S. multinational banks have become more leery about their lending practices, Iceland—a nation with 304,000 people, the same population as Pittsburgh—has found itself in a severe cash crunch of its own, a disturbing turn of events that has led some analysts to call the nation "the Bear Stearns of the North Atlantic." As James Surowiecki wrote in the *New Yorker:* "Iceland's current woes teach a useful lesson about the interconnectedness of global markets: trouble can come from anywhere. Homeowners default on mortgages in San Diego, and suddenly people in Reykjavik are paying more for gasoline and wondering if their bank deposits are safe."[11]

The real lesson of Iceland's predicament is that Iceland is not alone in borrowing recklessly from global investors. Surowiecki points to the billions of dollars in U.S. securities and currency held by Japan and China in particular. With the uncertainty about additional liabilities, financial institutions are unsure of their asset levels, creating surprises about what liquidity is available. On December 7, 2007, for example, when the Swiss Bank UBS rocked stock exchanges with its surprise $10 billion write-down on subprime exposure, the markets expected more unknown future write-offs, distorting the supply of funds. (The total write-downs at UBS were $38 billion over a four-month period, as of April 2008 and at the time of this printing.) With unknown supply and demand figures reverberating in markets far and near from the original transaction, volatility soars and economies shake.

Realities of Increased Volatility and Inflation

"Until the last moment," the Dalai Lama says, "Anything is possible."[12]

Volatility implies the potential for change—and it often requires courage to embrace such change instead of running from it. It's not just American investors who pounce on the opportunities created by volatile conditions: investors from countries such as South Korea, Canada, and Russia spent more than $414 billion in both private and public deals in 2007 to acquire everything from stocks in American companies to steel-making plants and baby food manufacturing facilities.[13] Usually these investments benefit both the investors and the host country where the jobs are located. Suppliers and employees have more stability when working with or for companies that attract investment capital. Approximately five million Americans work for foreign-owned companies based in the United States.

The market depends on individual transactions produced by people making rational self-interested decisions. Not surprisingly, a market works to the benefit of both parties in the transaction, often benefiting third parties as well. Volatility is not an indication that we need to limit or retreat from market forces. The market always presents opportunities as well as risks.

Volatility creates uncertainties and often drives prices up, as business agents on both sides of a contract or purchase agreement try to build-in a financial cushion to protect their respective profit margins from eroding. In the worst extreme, hoarding of commodities may occur, exacerbating the shortage of the raw materials or the products derived from the commodities. This in turn, may increase prices. In response, protectionists call for government action to control the market. If government bodies interfere and try to manage the prices through expanding the money supply, more currency chases the same amount of goods. If not managed well, excessive money supply and uncertainties can create hyperinflationary economies. Economists define *hyperinflation* as: "an inflationary cycle without any tendency toward equilibrium. Although there is a great deal of debate about the root causes of hyperinflation, it becomes visible when there is an unchecked increase in the money supply or drastic debasement of coinage, and is often associated with wars (or their aftermath), economic depressions, and political or social upheavals."[14] For example, Brazilians had to deal with hyperinflation from 1986 to 1994 when the country's military dictatorship adjusted the base currency three times in an attempt to deal with inflation.

The ripples that result from seemingly unconnected events, like the price of oil affecting the price of food, often have an unintended result: market volatility shaking consumers' and employers' confidence. And market volatility is not exclusive to the United States. According to the Conference Board, this is a global concern with both consumer and CEO confidence levels fluctuating around the world.[15] As the group reported in its 2007 annual report: "It's a volatile time for corporate leaders, who operate in a disruptive global environment in which the playing field constantly shifts, in which boards are less and less reticent [sic, reluctant] to change the

occupant of the corner office, in which different constituencies—from institutional investors to the business press—make
strong and often contradictory demands. The looming shortage of
young corporate stars will only widen the existing leadership gap."[16]

When fear and uncertainty begin to dominate the financial
climate, many leaders begin to over-correct and, consequently, make
poor decisions. In the past, news of a tragedy such as the 2004 Indian
Ocean tsunami or the April 1988 attack on a missile frigate in the
Strait of Hormuz might take days or weeks before it made headlines.
Today, news travels at the speed of the Internet—and bad news
in particular has the ability to cause panic almost instantaneously,
leading to reactions that have unforeseen consequences.

The losses to the American economy resulting from the 2001
terrorist attack on the World Trade Center in New York occurred
largely as a result of investor panic and business leader retrenchment. The stock market plummeted and investor confidence declined. President George W. Bush may well have issued one of his
most insightful messages of his tenure in office when, just after the
attack, he encouraged Americans to shop and make purchases. Too
many economic actors react adversely to what is perceived to be
threatening news. This adverse reaction, or panic, can have dire
consequences for an economy.

Volatility can be a harbinger of opportunity for those leaders
willing to look past their fears. Consider the temperamental reaction
of the U.S. stock market surrounding the actions of the Federal
Reserve to help salvage the remains of the investment bank Bear
Stearns in the first quarter of 2008. The rapid collapse of Bear
Stearns resulted from a lack of transparency about the status of
its assets, which led investors and regulators alike to rapidly lose
confidence in its liquidity. Some nervous investors perceived the
Bear Stearns tragedy as possibly the first in a row of dominoes to
fall.[17] While much of the news focused on the downside of the
big swings in the market caused by this company's bankruptcy, the
bigger story should have been that many investors jumped in to take
advantage of these swings to snap up bargains. Just a few weeks after
the storm cleared, the Dow Jones industrial average recovered more
than 350 points and stocks in the financial sector actually surged 10

percent in value.[18] Investors often welcome such volatility because it not only creates bargains, it also scares away potential competing bids. An open, free market helps give expression to the different points of view for those who want to sell and those who want to buy on bad news and creates a market for trading. In the twenty-first century, these decisions are increasingly being made based on worldwide news events and are expressed in a worldwide market, twenty-four hours by seven days.

Embracing volatility, therefore, means accepting the notion of "creative destruction," the term coined by economist Joseph Schumpeter in 1942 in his seminal work, *Capitalism, Socialism and Democracy*, which showed how capitalism, by its very nature, requires change, often by replacing the old with the new.[19] Schumpeter saw economies operating in cycles. Entrepreneurs initially break through the resistance of incumbent interests and pave the road for first movers. The resulting innovations boost prices and profits, which signals a cycle of prosperity. The resulting profits, however, attract imitators and overproduction, which eventually leads to an economic downswing. The resulting recession actually serves a Darwinian function, weeding out weaker competitors and setting the stage for a new wave of innovation that creates another economic upswing. When you look at volatility as a whole, therefore, the leaders who stand out are those who can put changes into a rational context and make the best decisions—leading their organizations into the next cyclical upturn.

Knowing When to Place Your Bets

Taking aggressive action in volatile environments not only requires courage, it also requires distinguishing good opportunities from bad ones. It strikes me that those individuals who make career changes after a successful track record in one career have the temerity to take advantage of fruitful opportunities. Herb Greenberg, the longtime columnist for the *Wall Street Journal*, decided in April 2008 to leave journalism to begin his own research firm during one of the more volatile markets in recent history.[20] In his sendoff column, Mr. Greenberg shared his five tips for developing timely insight to help you move in one direction while your competitors mistakenly move toward the other:

1. *The numbers don't lie.* Make your bets based on an analysis of numbers, not the statements or personal pledges from management that tries to spin the results.

2. *Quality of earnings, not quantity.* The real story is told in the balance sheet and cash flow statement, not the earnings projections and reports. The earnings are based on judgment calls and estimates and can be complex and convoluted. Understand how the business generates cash.

3. *Don't confuse stocks and companies.* Make your bets based on facts about the company, not on trends in its stock performance. Bets you place on upward trends tend to reverse themselves in a hurry.

4. *Risk isn't a four-letter word.* Smart investors understand how much they can afford to lose before they think about how much the share price will increase.

5. *GAAP isn't the same as a Good Housekeeping seal.* Even if a company presents its performance through a set of audited financials, there is still plenty of gray area for management to fudge earnings.

What's interesting is that Mr. Greenberg didn't even touch on a critical point about generally accepted accounting principles (GAAP) in general: that it is already being replaced around the world with a new standard—international financial reporting standards (IFRS). More on that in the next section.

New Realities of Financial Reporting

A new language for reporting and understanding financial results is now emerging. It's called the international financial reporting standards (IFRS). While U.S.-based companies still report their financials using generally accepted accounting principles (GAAP), companies around the world have been moving toward the new IFRS standards, which were developed between 1973 and 2001 by the International Accounting Standards Committee (IASC).[21] IASC developed a global accounting standard to replace the various versions of GAAP around the world, with their many different accounting rules. At the time this book went to press, more than 100 countries had adopted IFRS as their required reporting standard, with several large countries, such as Japan and Canada, planning to do so by 2011. As a result of U.S. GAAP and IFRS convergence over the next few years, we will have one universal economic reporting standard throughout the world that will facilitate trade, investments, and transparency of business results.

Mind the GAAP

One of the first tasks I undertook when I joined Sara Lee Corporation in the 1990s was to conduct due diligence on an acquisition target located in Finland. Our corporate development department was keen on closing the deal quickly. I felt pressure to find reasons to support the proposed deal as negotiated in the letter of intent. As Herb Greenberg advises, I analyzed and challenged assumptions to find out whether we had accurately assessed the value of this target company. And what I found shook me: the company had reported its financials under Finnish GAAP standards, which are different from U.S. GAAP standards. The corporate development folks had overvalued the potential target because they weren't using the correct language to evaluate excess and obsolete inventory valuations. While it was too late to back out of the deal completely, we did reduce our losses by buying a minority stake in the firm instead. The lesson learned is that the financial results a company reports may be subject to local rules and differ significantly from the GAAP with which you are familiar. It is primarily for this reason that a true global economic standard like IFRS is so clearly needed.

Learn More

For short summaries of all IFRS standards, news, and status of projects in progress, visit the IASB's web site at: www.iasb.org. For a roundup of case studies on the nations that have successfully adopted IFRS, visit the web site for the United Nations Conference on Trade and Development at: www.unctad.org. Also, KPMG, PricewaterhouseCoopers, Deloitte, and Ernst & Young have excellent information available to help investors and finance leaders understand the impact of convergence for specific industries and its implications.

Without going into significant detail, there are many differences between IFRS and U.S. GAAP, including everything from revenue recognition to the measurement dates of employee-based compensation to the taxing of intercompany profits. Each country's standard is like a different language and requires a translator to make an apples-to-apples comparison of how a company might be valued based on the standard used in reporting results. The benefits of adopting IFRS include comparability with international competitors, streamlined reporting for companies with global operations and foreign reporting requirements, and easier access to foreign investments and capital markets.

Management teams at many companies still don't see any good reason to switch from GAAP to IFRS even when they admit GAAP is a more onerous rule-based system rather than a principles-based one. Perhaps more pointedly, there aren't many accounting professionals that understand IFRS because most U.S. universities don't teach it. In the United States, colleges and universities are teaching U.S. GAAP accounting for an IFRS world. *Our future leaders will be armed with obsolete accounting and financial information before they even enter the workforce.* Revenue recognition and the manner in which companies report their profits will change. According to a survey of technology firms reported in CFO.com, 50 percent of the respondents felt that the Securities and Exchange Commission has penalized them for not forcing international firms to report their results according to U.S. GAAP.[22] With extended licensing agreements, technology companies using IFRS can recognize revenue more quickly upfront, while U.S. GAAP filers would have to recognize the revenue based on the terms of the arrangement, which might vary. But this line of thinking is outdated in the interconnected globe. The United States is now the outlier. Company leaders who insist on taking up defensive positions related to outdated accounting reporting standards will fall behind not only because they inaccurately value their own company, but also because they inaccurately value their competition. Foreign—and eventually domestic investors—will lose confidence in companies that don't report with IFRS.

Forward-thinking companies are making the change, even one step at a time. One early adopter of IFRS, E.ON, the largest industrial company in Germany at the end of December 2007 based on market capitalization, found that linking performance bonus computations to the IFRS reports quickened the adoption of IFRS in the U.S. subsidiary. For regulatory reasons, the company must still produce U.S. GAAP reporting of results, but management focuses on the results as reported under IFRS standards.

Robert Herz, Financial Accounting Standards Board (FASB) chairman, has called for a time line to move U.S. companies to the IFRS standard because it is quickly becoming the global standard for accounting principles.[23] As an American who lived in England and Argentina, Mr. Herz understands the importance of seeing business through a global lens. He is a zealot for IFRS and endorses convergence. Courageous leaders will recognize this trend and help push their organizations forward to take advantage of the opportunities it will create. Perhaps the top priority for in-house training in the next two or three years is an intense program for all financial people in IFRS.

Fortunately, there are leaders at some U.S.-based companies who are moving aggressively to become IFRS-compliant, not because they see it as a threat, but because they think they can create new opportunities and even expose potential threats from competitors using comparable metrics. One exemplary company is the railway division of shipping and transportation giant, Norfolk Southern

Corp.[24] You can't think of a more domestic, land-locked company than Norfolk Southern, which operates about 21,500 miles of track in 22 U.S. states. With six major railroad companies in North America, Norfolk Southern meets regularly at rail conferences to discuss industry-wide issues. At the May 2008 conference, the company's leaders were actively involved with determining the right time to switch to the new accounting standard and in a manner in synch with their industry. Norfolk Southern is evaluating the adoption of IFRS for public reporting and for access to capital. Their corporate controller, Marta Stewart, recognized that one of the major changes will be mark-to-market valuations each quarter for their pension plan assets and liabilities. Such valuations determine the value of a financial instrument based on the current market price and will fluctuate as open markets fluctuate. "We want the ground to settle" before we make the change and begin training.[25] Norfolk Southern's leaders understand that to fit into the global marketplace and attract international investors, they will need to communicate externally and internally for a smooth convergence of U.S. GAAP and IFRS reporting.

New Realities of the Global Enterprise

In a world with just one time zone—now—business must source materials, innovation, talent, logistics, infrastructure, and production wherever they are best available.

—Yang Yuanqing, Chairman of the Board, Lenovo[26]

As Norfolk Southern demonstrates, the new realities created by changes in supply and demand, volatility, and financial reporting force organizations to transform themselves into one of Peter Drucker's "transnational companies."[27] Global trade now makes up about half of global GDP and deeper economic bonds continue to link the developed and developing worlds, as evidenced by an increase in both the number of cross-border merger and acquisition

(M&A) deals as well as the amount of cross-border foreign direct investment.[28]

Companies that fail to "go global" also risk leaving enormous opportunities on the table. Economic growth in Brazil, Russia, India, and China—the so-called BRIC nations—could be quadruple the GDP increases of the collective G6 nations—France, Germany, Japan, United Kingdom, Italy and the United States—over the next 40 years.[29] And, when you look at how trade between developing and industrialized nations has evolved over the past decade, you begin to see how much has changed. In short, the developing world has begun cultivating trading partners apart from what we now know as the industrialized nations. As Figures 2.2 and 2.3 illustrate, emerging markets have accelerated trade with developed markets at the same time the percentage of developed markets trade with emerging markets have plunged.

The rise of emerging markets isn't limited to just the BRIC nations, as economic growth in countries like South Korea, Mexico, Singapore, and Turkey, among others, exceeds the growth rates of developed economies. Some of the growth rates are computed on

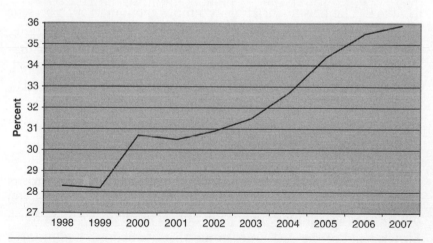

Figure 2.2 Trade with Developing Nations (as a Share of Total Trade by Industrial Nations) *Data source:* International Monetary Fund, www.imfstatistics.org/DOT/ (subscription required).

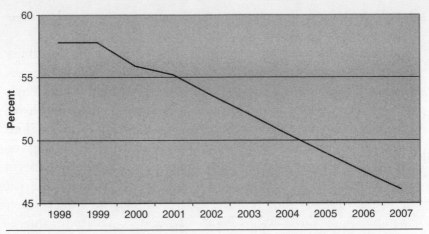

Figure 2.3   Trade with Industrial Nations (as a Share of Total Trade by Developing Nations) *Data source:* International Monetary Fund, www.imfstatistics.org/DOT/ (subscription required).

a small base, but that does not contradict the point. These emerging economies result from their burgeoning populations, new open market legislation, and revitalized industrial and service delivery capabilities. The new financial opportunities these markets represent require all companies to think and act globally. The rise of emerging markets creates similar big opportunities for the leaders of companies whether based in Vietnam, Germany, or Ireland, to name a few. The consulting firm Accenture notes that emerging-market multinationals (EMMs), companies based in emerging markets with operations in more than one country, are expanding at a rapid rate.[30] The Fortune 500 now includes more than 70 companies based in emerging markets—up from just 20 in 1998. To spur growth, these companies have also invested heavily in expansion to new markets and in mergers and acquisitions. They conducted more than 1,100 transactions worth more than $128 billion in 2006 alone. As Mark Foster, head of the Accenture group that studied the rise of these EMMs, writes: "In many respects, multinationals are a defining invention of Western economies. But like much else in the multi-polar world, they are no longer the preserve of the West. The rapidly growing emerging economies are producing business giants of their own at a staggering rate."[31]

The investment bank Goldman Sachs has also studied the performance of what it calls "GloCo" (Global Companies)—27 companies including British Petroleum, General Electric, PetroChina, and Volkswagen—that met Goldman Sach's criteria as an organization equipped to tackle the challenges of the global economy.[32] The eight criteria used to identify GloCo were that they:

1. Focus on globalization as critical to the company's future.
2. Have a global brand.
3. Are seen as a local firm in the local market.
4. Demonstrate flexibility.
5. Use technology to advance the business.
6. Have employee-friendly workplace practices.
7. Have a strategy for China and other major developing countries.
8. Have meaningful social engagement at the local level.

The researchers found that GloCo collectively outperformed their local equity indices by more than 8 percent between 1996 and 2005—indicating that investors are attuned to the advantages offered by companies capable of tapping into global opportunities. In pursuing global leadership positions, these companies gained access to new markets, new technologies, a global workforce, inexpensive transport and communications, as well as a fresh approach to doing business. The researchers also concluded that, in order to confront future challenges, meeting the eight criteria wasn't enough. To compete successfully, would-be global companies need to focus on building five key relationships: with employees, consumers, local communities, governments, and investors. As the researchers concluded: "With each of these groups, GloCo must forcefully argue the case for globalization, showing that it helps the greater good as well as the bottom line. GloCo need to demonstrate that globalization is likely to yield broad and sustainable benefits, including wider consumer choice, greater opportunity, economic development and more inclusive governance structures. It is in GloCo's own self-interest to pursue these challenges with vigor."

To pursue these challenges, therefore, organizations from around the globe need to cultivate the kinds of leaders capable of pushing ahead and tackling these new opportunities. To help you prioritize your actions, consider the view of one of the experts on global trends and strategic advice. Ambassador Charlene Barshefsky, formerly the U.S. Trade Representative and chief trade negotiator for the United States from 1996 to 2001, is best known for negotiating the historic market opening agreement with China on its entry to the World Trade Organization. She sees three apparent trends: First, the rise of other countries developing at a high GDP growth rate will dilute the economic effect the United States has enjoyed and used in negotiations. This has substantial implications on business as the traditional competitive weight and heft from the United States shifts to the rest of the world. Second, the population growth of Muslim Asia and about one-half of the continent of Africa will have business implications. Most poor, unstable, and weak states that are suffused with radical ideology will call U.S. power into question in many ways. Third, climate change will accelerate the trend of the greatest global intervention of governments and bureaucracy the business world has experienced, except during major wartime. Climate is the biggest single threat to the stability and continued economic development of the multi-polar world because populations will migrate to seek water and clean air. She argues that as migration occurs, politicians will intensify the debate over the autonomy of countries with regards to their borders, both with the United States and around the globe.[33] Now, more than ever, we need courageous and talented leaders who can deal with these forces to open a market economy before we experience an open political economy. The rise of emerging countries and their view on market economics will matter now and in the future as the U.S. domination and ability to keep those markets open and functioning are eroding. A strategy for private and public partnerships will become critical as these three trends affect companies across national borders.

Key Points to Consider

When thinking about the new financial realities of the interconnected globe, ask the following questions:

- Given the realities of supply and demand, are there opportunities for your organization that you may have overlooked? How about threats?

- How can you shape your organization's ability to prepare for and respond to volatility?

- How do you evaluate investments and reconcile the external financial reports with what management proclaims the results are?

- Can you be the key driver to bring your organization into the global market through IFRS?

- What big-bet effort can you initiate or support to help your organization take advantage of opportunities to build relationships with its constituencies before a crisis occurs?

Taking the Next Steps on Your Journey

Knowing that the economic tectonic plates are shifting between countries and continents started our journey. This led to the awareness that new financial rules will be necessary to navigate in markets in order to understand the results of strategies. It is one thing to understand the rules and language of business. It is another to find the right people who have the passion to engage others and pursue global opportunities. The ways of doing business in different cultures may vary, but there are critical leadership skills required to keep progressing and not become overwhelmed. The next chapter addresses who you should attract and how to define the leadership capabilities required when the globe is shaking.

Four Types of Leaders

When I moved to Portland, Maine, from Chicago, Illinois, in 1994, I thought I had moved to a different country. Of course, the basic English language and currency were the same. But the customs and values of the leaders in Portland were different from those in Chicago to which I had been accustomed. In fact, during my first year in Maine, I did not take any of my usual trips outside of the United States. Instead, I immersed myself in the culture of Maine and worked to acquaint myself with business leaders in the community while I integrated myself into the Fortune 500 company for which I worked. In other words, I studied the local norms and the business environment and adapted myself to it.

I had a lot to learn. Fortunately, the company for which I worked already had in place state-of-the-art sourcing and logistics systems that accessed products from around the world and distributed them quickly and inexpensively. Our interconnected world demands leaders who understand the essential dynamics of business systems. Leaders who have integration and transformation skills are well positioned to achieve business results. Integration is the ability to connect with unfamiliar people and cultures—to identify the important, often unstated and informal, norms and behaviors of cultures so that various talents and people with different points of view work efficiently and achieve the business objectives. Transformation is the process of creating institutional change for both short-term and long-term benefit. Transformation allows a company to be relevant by adapting to new conditions. In the twenty-first century, those new conditions often arise globally and a transformative company must change in accordance with those global situations. The willingness to accept change and embrace transformation enables leaders to set themselves apart from their peers. Leaders use change to create innovative products and services, enter new markets, and adopt new skills and competencies. The old pace of change from a few years ago looks nothing like today's velocity of change arising from sudden exigencies from multiple evident and hidden sources. The rise in the number of anonymous bloggers or whistle blowers, protected from recrimination as a result of laws, gives voice to many people who in the past would have remained silent. These voices provide early warning signals to a company. But anonymity can also create undesired viral attacks and could lend credence to suspicion based on inconclusive evidence or innuendo. Initiating change requires an often-elusive component in leadership: courage to assume responsibility.

Courageous Leadership in Action

Courage is different from bravery; and in a business context, this difference is magnified. Courage implies firmness of mind and will in the face of danger or extreme difficulty.[1] A leader with courage possesses a mindset that allows himself or herself to respond to crises that he or she may not have sought, but which were nonetheless presented. In my life, I have often encountered courageous business leaders when I, too, have had to make a courageous stand. One such example occurred when I met John Bryan, the former Chairman and CEO of Sara Lee Corporation, in 1990. At that time I was an employee of Kraft Foods. An executive search firm contacted me about a desirable global position at Sara Lee. After successful interviews for the position, the recruiter said I could not continue the interview process because Kraft Foods was a competitor involved in litigation with Sara Lee. Kraft had recently sued Sara Lee to prevent it from hiring a key research and development scientist. I was particularly attracted to Sara Lee because the company was beginning to invest heavily in new markets outside the United States. I wanted to be a part of that transformation. You can imagine my disappointment when I realized that the recruitment process was coming to an abrupt end. Yet, a week after learning that I would not be able to complete the last step in the interview process, which included meeting John Bryan, a new door fortuitously opened. As a member of the Chicago Council of Foreign Relations, I read that John would be speaking at a lunch on the future of the food business around the world. I made sure that I attended and, at the end of the session, introduced myself and explained my disappointment not to have the chance to work together. I'm not exactly sure what happened next except that the recruiters called and told me the interview was back on.

I started at Sara Lee in early 1991 and during my first week on the job went to France to attend strategy meetings to determine which companies in Europe we wanted to acquire. Three months after that, I was working in Finland conducting due diligence on an acquisition the corporate development department desperately wanted. My findings, however, showed that the financial evaluation model the team was using was badly flawed. By September, I decided that we should terminate the deal. Because of legal constraints, we were forced to at least buy a minority position in the Finnish company. John Bryan later told me that it took courage to speak up to make an unpopular recommendation. He told me that he appreciated what I had done to save the company from wasting money and incurring the large losses that would have resulted if we had proceeded to buy the company's entire operations. I will never forget his support and his words of wisdom. He told me that his courage came from doing what is right, even in the face of strong opposition and expectations. I had a new appreciation for the course of events that had brought me to Sara Lee. John was courageous enough to risk a lawsuit over hiring me away from Kraft. These were hardly isolated instances of John's courage. The French people recognized his leadership when they awarded him the *Légion d'Honneur*, the highest civilian honor they can bestow on a foreigner.[2]

Courage Quotient

John Bryan is a great example of a courageous leader. Over the years, I have searched for an analytic measurement to identify other leaders with similar qualities—no matter what country or organization that leader calls home. During my research and working with professionals in the field of human resources, I learned what separates leaders like John and others like him from those leaders who, because they lack courage, eschew new roads as too risky or too often see obstacles rather than opportunities.

From this research, my company developed, tested, and fielded the CQ Assessment Tool.[®3] The assessment probes a person's willingness to take risks while conforming to the corporate culture in which he finds himself. When we analyze the results, we find that leaders like John, who have both the ability to integrate and transform organizations, all have something in common: a high *courage quotient* (CQ). While we know that the intelligence quotient—IQ—deals with the mind, and the emotional quotient—EQ—deals with feelings, CQ deals with the spirit. CQ measures an individual's drive and perception of his organization. It captures a critical third element that allows us to better understand why some people with high a IQ and EQ succeed and others stop trying. A courageous leader has the additional ability to stand out at the opportune moment. While individuals who have a *sense of curiosity* turn emotions and ideas into action and those who have an *emphatic sense* spur collaboration and the cultivation of relationships around them, courageous leaders inspire those around them to tackle bold, new opportunities. Two other factors that drive a leader's CQ are *competence* and *perseverance:* the abilities to drive accomplishment through hard work and innovation combined with a desire for continual self-improvement.

Leaders with high CQ scores are effective at standing out by moving their organization toward new opportunities that create long-term value for all stakeholders. In addition, they understand how to work with others within their organization—navigating the political and operating systems—to get things done in the face of obstacles, criticism, or even in the wake of their own mistakes.

What Is Your CQ Score?

While courage is important for any business leader, it is especially important for global business leaders. Working with multiple cultures, economies, currencies, laws, and regulations—all within a realm of heightened geopolitical tension—creates tremendous uncertainty. Even the brightest and most experienced business leaders cannot have firsthand knowledge of the intricacies of multiple foreign cultures, their laws, and economic policies. Actively seeking input from employees and advisors, knowing one's own values and convictions, and synthesizing the risks and opportunities requires thoughtful action. This is courage.

There are things that each of us can do to become more courageous, and thereby become better able to compete successfully in a global marketplace. First, each individual must have an objective awareness of his or her own level of courage. A leader's courage can be estimated with the help of the CQ Assessment Tool. A series of quantitative and qualitative questions measure a leader's potential to fit in by measuring the level of collaboration (based on *integrative* skills) with which the individual is comfortable. A leader's ability to stand out is assessed by measuring the level of risk (based on *transformative* skills) that the individual is willing to take.[4]

A leader's CQ score is driven by his or her ability to both *Fit In* and to *Stand Out*—skills we can measure quantitatively and assess. The *Fit In* (integrative) measures are financial acuity, integrity, and linkages. Financial acuity, that is, understanding how the company makes money and measures its financial success, builds confidence.

Integrity, doing the right things in the right way in order to preserve the reputation of the company, creates stakeholder trust. Linkages, working to build and leverage a wide and effective network of stakeholders in order to provide access to new people and new ways of thinking, open the door to opportunity.

The *Stand Out* (transformative) measures are learning, perspective, and global citizenship. Learning, being continuously open to new disciplines and ideas, fosters creativity and innovation. Perspective, developing and sharing insight that raises the performance bar personally and professionally for an individual and collectively for the organization, is critical to bringing balanced judgment into decision making. Global citizenship, the ability to think broadly and operate in a world that is increasingly interconnected and interdependent, creates the skill of flexibility and adaptability to uncertain environments. This leads to mental agility.

My company conducted a survey to identify characteristics of who would most likely be the courageous prototype.[5] This survey included men and women from three different generations (Baby Boomers, Generation X, and Generation Y). And when we analyzed the results, we found that four factors correlated to a high CQ score.

The first factor we identified was that respondents who showed confidence in managing money, such as having control of a budget, received high CQ scores. Of the 41 percent of the survey's respondents that controlled some portion of their organization's expenses, more than half received CQ scores of 7 or higher (on a scale from 1 to 10). This result suggests that financial acuity is a key factor in both the ability to Fit It, and Stand Out.

Second, quick thinkers who make fast decisions also had high CQ scores. One hypothesis for this result is that as a person makes more decisions in the same amount of time, he or she develops a capability and willingness to take risks. As an individual gains experience and confidence, he or she can then make decisions in a fast-paced environment. Plus, if the decision happens to be the wrong one, that individual, because of his or her ability to adjust, would then be able to make a correction through a subsequent decision.

The third factor we identified was related to communication style: the 51 percent of respondents who reported that they relied on direct and open communication received higher CQ scores than those who employed careful and closed communication. These results are supported by the fact that open communication allows for the free flow of information, which leads to informed decisions and new perspectives. Individuals who have access to the right information also have higher confidence in themselves and the validity of their choices.

The fourth factor we identified was that the highest CQ scores belonged to women born between 1975 and 1985 (late Generation X, early Generation Y). This result may be explained by the fact that women tend to use open communication more than men and tend to take decisive action more quickly—in addition to possessing financial acuity. It may also be due to the tendency of this generation to move back home where the safety net provided by their parents emboldens their actions. There may be a maturity factor in this age group where some people have enough experience without having outdated technical skills. A combination of these factors leads to courageous actions.

If we plot these results from the CQ Assessment Tool on a matrix, we can segment the group of leaders into four distinct quadrants: Conventional, Compliant, Challenger, and Courageous (see Figure 3.1).

To better understand each type, we'll look at case studies illustrating how these leaders might act in the interconnected world.

Conventional

The *conventional* leader is a person who wants a "club" culture, someone who wants to live his or her passion outside of work and is reluctant to alter his or her own status quo, let alone the world. The conventional leader scores high on the *Fit In* dimension and low on the *Stand Out* dimension. This profile suggests that the individual is capable of collaborating with stakeholders to get things done but lacks the risk orientation that drives higher levels of performance. The conventional leader can be helpful in implementing current

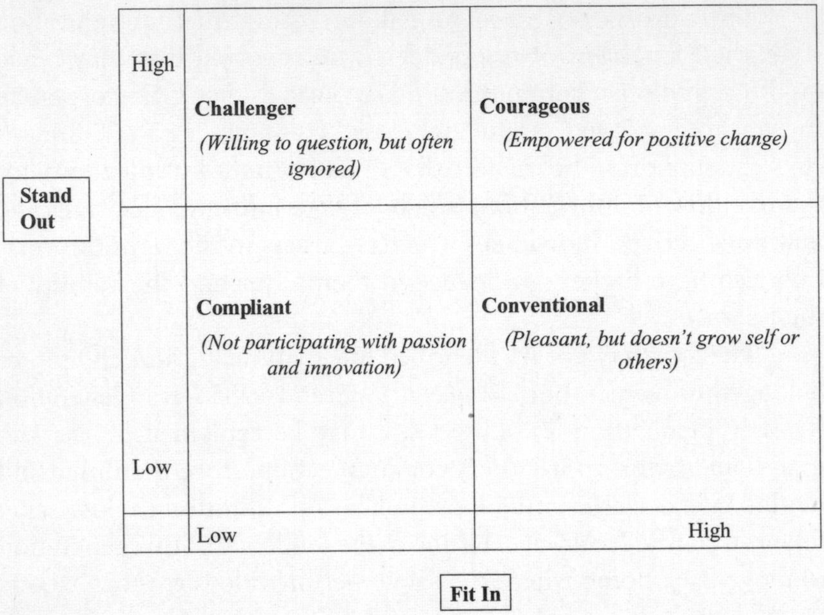

Figure 3.1   Four Kinds of Leaders

strategies but will not demonstrate the risk orientation needed to raise the performance bar and develop innovative strategies and plans. If you are conventional, you need to determine whether low engagement with your work will provide you with the economic wherewithal and intellectual growth you will need to survive in this global marketplace.

Case Study of Conventional Leadership

Michael Lewis, the best-selling author and former Wall Street trader, wrote an article called "The New Organization Man." Lewis was, in essence, writing an obituary for the seemingly humorless and mindlessly loyal workers of the 1950s made famous by novels like Sloan Wilson's *The Man in the Gray Flannel Suit* and William H. Whyte's treatise, *The Organization Man.*[6] As Lewis writes about these participants in the "deplorable, metronomic life of the American businessman":

He commuted to work in his immaculate gray suit every day from his neat suburban tract house. He kept his front lawn and his hair trimmed to lengths tacitly agreed upon by his peers. He avoided high culture, and anything else that smacked of elitism. He embraced the personality tests administered to him by his corporate employers. These tests plumbed the depths of his willingness to conform.

Though Lewis argues that this Organization Man is dead, replaced by a younger generation of entrepreneurial risk takers, I would counter that we all know current or former coworkers who seem to know how to do enough not to get fired. Some people are so eager to be part of a group; they don't want to try a new approach and risk being wrong. While you might have enjoyed a conversation with a pleasant chap at lunch, at the end of the day you wonder what he accomplished. Or, possibly you're reminded of the coworker who spent more time seeking approval than he or she ever did seeking out new opportunities. While these conventional thinkers can make good teammates, since, given a specific task, they can complete it, they are also incapable of pushing a team to higher levels if thrust into a leadership role. The key in grooming conventional leaders to become courageous ones is to encourage these individuals to push themselves and their ambition—to have the courage to take some risks in order to break free from the routines of the Organization Man.

Compliant

A *compliant* leader wants to show up for work, collect a paycheck, and focus more on what has been, rather than what is or will be. A compliant leader keeps his team or himself using past practices that may have become antiquated or may no longer work given new management or new competition. Such a leader scores low on both the *Fit In* dimension and the *Stand Out* dimension. This profile suggests that the individual neither has an appropriate focus on collaborating nor will take prudent risks in order to support the strategies and goals of the organization. The individual may agree to follow the rules and plans, and then proceed to do something quite different. If you are compliant, you must determine if you lack motivation due to temporal distractions and priorities or if you don't have the capability to function in your current role. You may be in special circumstances, but you may be at risk of losing your job in an economic downturn.

A Case Study of Compliant Leadership

Another result of the interconnected globe is that you can't hide from your mistakes by moving to a new company or new country. One of the first things I do to learn more about a person is search the Internet. I find this extra step provides some insight into that person's character and personal interests. The compliant leader can sometimes find himself in a situation where he should have spoken up and stood out. A brief blurb in the *New York Times* last year noted that Mr. X, a former Enterasys finance executive, had been sentenced to nine years in prison.[7] This bit of news immediately caught my attention because Mr. X used to work for me. Though he had been at the company for 10 years, rising to the position of corporate controller, I ended up firing him, in part for what I believed to be his lack of courage. At one important audit committee meeting he said he was going to do one thing, yet ended up doing something completely different. When I asked why and what happened, he told me the chairman was staring at him and he just couldn't help himself. He could not express a new and different approach that might challenge the chairman's assumptions. I had provided Mr. X a chance to impress company leadership with an innovative proposal and he backed away. While many might find a lack of courage to be considerably different from criminal ethics, it did not surprise me that the jury found Mr. X guilty of conspiracy, securities fraud, falsifying books and records of a public company, making false statements to the auditors, and, last but not least, wire fraud. It nonetheless saddened me that an otherwise bright individual had ruined his career and that the Internet would make his criminal conviction accessible to anyone in the world.

More important, I think Mr. X's actions illustrate what happens when leaders think and act compliantly. In part because such individuals are focused more on themselves than on their teammates, their ambition is often curtailed in favor of acting out of self-preservation. Whereas *conventional* leaders at least have the skill to fit in, *compliant* leaders lack the capability to *Stand Out* or *Fit In*. Such individuals, as we can see from the conclusion to Mr. X's story, can therefore be particularly damaging to an organization and should be removed with haste.

Challenger

The people in the *challenger* role are often younger, eager workers with high expectations who want to succeed and make a difference. Yet, they are deficient in knowing the "hidden rules" or hidden hierarchies in business. They need to learn these rules to truly create an effective and collaborative team. The challenger leader scores low on the *Fit In* dimension and high on the *Stand Out* dimension of the FISO Index. This profile suggests that the individual has the perspective and risk orientation to make innovative and perhaps even breakthrough contributions. However, the individual seeks to impose his or her point of view on others without understanding the full situation and others' points of view. If you are a challenger, you need to develop collaboration skills. Even the best ideas may not be developed if you cannot work jointly with others to convert the intellectual endeavor to meaningful results. You may be in the wrong position and may need to find a job inside or outside your organization that allows you to work better with colleagues, bosses, subordinates, suppliers, customers, investors, or the constituency necessary for you to accomplish your job responsibilities.

A Case Study of a Challenger in Action

One of the more publicized meltdowns between a chief executive and her board in recent years involved Cara "Carly" Fiorina, the former CEO of computer maker Hewlett-Packard.[8] After the board fired Fiorina, it became evident that she had different strategic objectives concerning the acquisition of Compaq and that her communication style did not fit in with the culture of the company and the board. Lacking the key capability of fitting in ultimately led to her losing her position as one of the most influential executives in the world.

No one can argue that Fiorina's rise to the top was anything less than astronomical. After receiving her MBA in 1980, she went to work for AT&T as a management trainee. I recently attended a conference where Fiorina was the keynote speaker and she reflected on this time, when she was having difficulty making the transition into the corporate world. In particular, she mentioned how daunting one particular class project that involved role-playing seemed to her: "Why was I afraid? I was afraid because I thought I might fail. I was afraid because I had never done it before. I was afraid because I thought I might look foolish. But I *was* afraid. One of the things that I know about people, about life, is that everybody is afraid of something, and fear gets in the way of people realizing their potential. Fear also gets in the way of people making the changes they need to make, whether it's in their own lives or in their organizations."

Fiorina, like other challengers, made it a priority to push ahead when more conventional or compliant leaders might have shied away. In particular, she has been a proponent of acting on the opportunities present in our interconnected world. She was clearly rewarded time and time again for those efforts. But perhaps that success clouded her ability to see her achievements for what they were: team efforts. Instead, she carried a high social profile where she was often seen mingling with the elite from Washington, DC, and Hollywood alike.

Her push to acquire Compaq is also an excellent case in point. Fiorina campaigned heavily for the acquisition even in the face of opposition from board members like Walter Hewlett, the son of HP founder William Hewlett. Like other challengers, Fiorina neglected to recognize parameters that exist within corporate or other cultures.

Changing cultures is a slow process and frequently depends on the ability to build consensus. Fiorina failed to persuade different constituencies how the acquisition would *Fit In*, at the same time she was pushing forward her agenda to *Stand Out*. One lesson evident in this example, therefore, is that challengers are particularly powerful assets to have within an organization—as long as there are efforts made to cultivate new skills to enable them to work within the team, not around it.

Courageous

The people in the *courageous* role, unlike the other prototypes, understand that it takes personal risk or sacrifice to make a difference. Their passions and energy are devoted to a cause. They possess a real desire to improve the future of their companies throughout their chosen parts of the globe. They recognize the key lesson that all employees must learn—that they have a value to an employer only so long as they serve that employer's needs and goals. The courageous leader scores high on the *Fit In* dimension and high on the *Stand Out* dimension. This profile suggests that the individual is capable of collaborating and willing to take risks in order to get short-term results and create long-term value. The courageous leader is a valued member of the organization and often serves as a pace setter for stimulating learning and change. Courageous leaders serve as both *thought catalysts* for change and as effective *change agents*. They are willing and able to take the risk required in change and willing and able to build the collaborative relationships that make performance sustainable. If you are courageous, you will be a role model and exemplify the values and actions appreciated by your organization.

You leverage your talents by developing other individuals for their future success.

A Case Study of Courageous Leadership

When I look back at my own career, no business leader's courage has had a bigger impact on me than John Bryan.[9] Though he is perhaps best known for serving as CEO of the Sara Lee Corp., he has also been a member of the board of directors for companies such as Bank One Corp., General Motors, Amoco, and Goldman Sachs. He's also been a key participant in the World Economic Forum held each year in Davos, Switzerland. Recently, he served as chairman for two major civic improvements in the city of Chicago—Millennium Park and the Modern Wing of the Art Institute of Chicago, with a fund-raising budget of more than $1 billion. He combines his local and global interests with his charitable interests and the restoration of his estate, a working farm.

Perhaps working on that farm symbolizes the closing of a loop. In order to accomplish all he has in his life, as a leader in the worlds of both business and philanthropy, Bryan had the courage to become a global citizen. Born in rural West Point, Mississippi, his family's company was sold to the conglomerate that became Sara Lee Corporation. He became CEO of the company at the age of 39 and served in that role and as chairman for 25 years. Bryan told me that growing up when Mississippi was evolving out of segregation was a major challenge. I recall a story he told me about how, as a young businessman working for his father's meat-packing plant, he learned that someone had dumped manure into a town pool in order to prevent interracial swimming. Bryan quickly mobilized an effort to raise money to clean the pool, only to be continually rebuffed by other folks in town who resisted the opening of a desegregated pool. He paid for the cleanup out of his own pocket and he was rewarded with a burning cross in his front yard.

Courage often means standing up for your beliefs even in the face of the most fearsome of naysayers. But, as Bryan continues to prove again and again, courage also involves empathy for others and a willingness to stand out when an opportunity to help others presents itself. As Bryan once told me, "The goal of philanthropy is to get your friends to give more money to your causes than you give to theirs."

Building Blocks of Courage

I truly believe that everyone has the potential to be a courageous leader. Obviously, some individuals will need to work harder than others to do so. Like learning any skill, a leader must study and exercise often to build his or her CQ muscle. Here are four building blocks of courage, along with some exceptional examples to encourage you to boost your own abilities as a leader.

1. Competence

When you think about the great achievers in the world today, it's hard to look past Oprah Winfrey's growing list of remarkable accomplishments.[10] Winfrey is best known for her award-winning television show, *The Oprah Winfrey Show*, which is the highest rated TV show in history and is watched each week by an estimated 46 million viewers from more than 134 countries around the world. But Winfrey hasn't stopped there. She launched a magazine, *O, The Oprah Magazine*; a production company, Harpo Productions, that has produced numerous award-winning TV shows and movies; and her web site, Oprah.com, whose most popular component may be Oprah's Book Club which, with more than one million members, is the largest book club in the world. Everything Winfrey touches, it seems, turns to gold. Yet, she rejects most of the opportunities extended to her to expand her brand. Rather than overextend herself, Winfrey makes sure that each endeavor she undertakes results in a major success.

Do you set the bar for your accomplishments high and find ways to tackle them realistically? The key to building a reputation for competence is to do what you say you're going to do—while building new capabilities for your organization in the process.

2. Curiosity

One of my favorite quotes is from Amar Bose, the founder of the company of the same name that designs the now world-famous sound systems. When asked about why he started his company, Bose replied: "I never went into business to make money. I went into business so that I could do interesting things that hadn't been done before."[11]

Bose, who was born in Philadelphia to an American mother, may have inherited some of his courage to pursue his interests from his father, Noni Gopal Bose, an Indian freedom revolutionary from Bengal who fled Calcutta in the 1920s to escape prosecution for his political activities. Amar Bose, who exhibited an aptitude for electronics at an early age when he, at the age of thirteen, started a business repairing radios and toy trains, attended MIT, where he eventually earned a PhD in electrical engineering. But it was his passion for music, specifically the challenge of building a speaker system that could replicate the visceral sound felt in a concert hall that led Bose down the path to fame and fortune. Today, tourists visiting the Sistine Chapel in Rome and astronauts blasting into space aboard the shuttle use Bose speakers and other patented technologies his company discovered and developed.

What drives the kinds of projects or responsibilities for which you strive? Are you receptive to new ideas, both your own and those originating from your colleagues? As you develop your listening and analytical skills and pursue your curiosity, you will be amazed at the new opportunities to be tapped.

3. Caring

Howard Schultz, chairman of Starbucks Coffee Company, decided to offer employee benefits to his employees no matter what business he ran because he was haunted by the memory of what happened to his father, who worked at low-paying jobs with little to show for it when he died. "He was beaten down, he wasn't respected," Schultz said. "He had no health insurance, and he had no workers' compensation when he got hurt on the job." So with Starbucks

Coffee Company, Schultz, "wanted to build the kind of company that my father never got a chance to work for, in which people were respected."[12]

When I met Howard Schultz a few years ago, he exuded a compassionate, caring nature. Always willing to listen to others, he also has firm convictions, whether it is that the New York Yankees should win the World Series or how to continually innovate for customers or what it takes to develop employees. He wants to have his employees care as much about the business as he does. He willingly takes the blame for bad ideas to create a safe environment for his employees to be creative. Schultz explained his mistakes, including his "brilliant idea to create a magazine, called Joe. ... We sold five copies in a month. ... We lost, again, millions of dollars, 'Howard's idea.' I keep a rack of the magazines at the bottom of my desk in a way to celebrate, not my mistake, but in a way to encourage our people to have the courage to not play it safe."[13]

4. Perseverance

When you think of perseverance, consider how hard professional athletes like Tiger Woods work to make what they do seem so easy. Tiger is clearly the most famous golfer in the world and, to some, the greatest player the game has ever seen.[14] Tiger was obviously born with an amazing gift not only to send a golf ball traveling more than 350 yards—he can also hit it exactly where he wants. But as the old saying goes: "You drive for show and you putt for dough," meaning championships are won on the greens, not in the air. And putting often takes practice—hours of it—to get a feel for the speed and angles of the closely cropped grass. To perfect his game, Tiger has been known to play 18 holes of golf the morning *before* he plays a major tournament, just to tune his game to its maximum level. Tiger also uses his practice time to gauge what components of his game are working—and which ones are not. Just as Tiger learns and adjusts after using the wrong club on an approach shot, we as leaders also need to learn from our mistakes—even if we have thousands of spectators dissecting every move we make.

Sometimes courage means having the drive to take on even the most daunting of tasks: admitting that we are wrong once in a while. But, courage also means not giving up in the face of high hurdles. Next time you're faced with an obstacle—whether that might be a sand trap or an unhappy board—square up and be prepared to give it your best shot.

Key Points to Consider

When assessing your own capabilities as a courageous leader, consider how your colleagues might evaluate you:

- How do you shape the discussion to energize the dialogue?
- Can you think of at least five people who would follow you to a new company or project? Do you actively seek to build relationships within your organization and find others who appreciate this?
- How often do colleagues seek your advice and follow it?
- When was the last time you recognized and thanked others who contributed to the success of your project or your job?
- How do you learn beyond your current ken? Do you consciously push yourself to learn and explore different cultures?

Now that we've addressed where the globe is interconnected, *why* courage is required given the financial realities derived from this interdependence in economies and the four ways of understanding *who* the global leaders are, it is time to explore further how you can adapt to these economic forces in various cultures. We begin our journey to explore the first of the six major forces—cultural norms—and how it shapes the multipolar world.

In order to *Shake the Globe*, leaders must focus particularly on understanding how to develop and shape courage related to our interconnected world. Let's move on to see how to do that.

Connecting the World in Six Stops

CHAPTER 4

Cultural Norms

Robert W. Fogel, who received a Nobel Prize in economics in 1993, predicts that global economic power will soon shift. In an article entitled "Capitalism and Democracy in 2040," Fogel writes that, "ever since World War II, the countries that have dominated the world economy"—principally the United States and European countries—"have shared a broad commitment to liberal and democratic values." But, when he compared the gross domestic products (GDPs) of nations in 2000 to their projected GDPs in 2040, Fogel saw many changes ahead. "The most striking feature is the relative decline in economic power of the EU 15 [15 countries in the European Union in 2000], implied by its stagnant population and its modest growth in GDP." The most startling prediction, though, is the forecast growth rate of different economies. Based on reasonable assumptions, the United States will grow its GDP at 3.8 percent, while the projected growth in the EU 15 is 1.2 percent, China is 8.4 percent and the entire world is 5.0 percent. Fogel argues that China will "go from a poor country in 2000 to a superrich country in 2040, although it will not have overtaken the United States." Where will the growth come from? New influential political and cultural factors are also emerging along with the changes to economic growth. Fogel believes that education, for one, is a key, noting that "college-educated workers are three times as productive as workers with less than a ninth-grade education, and high-school graduates are 1.8 times as productive."[1]

U.S. leaders generally have a formal education, but they need to expose themselves to perspectives outside of their own culture to compete in the global workforce. It's been my experience that we learn about our own prejudices, strengths and weaknesses, and limitations of knowledge when confronting a culture other than our own. There's no question that stepping into a new culture can be intimidating. Taking that first step to try and fit in can also present different challenges depending on your nation of origin. Talya Zemach-Bersin, a graduate of Wesleyan College in Middletown, Connecticut, touched on the mixed experience she had while studying abroad in Tibet in 2005. Talya describes the difficulties she encountered in "acting like the locals." While her college curriculum had focused on teaching her about the politics, economics, and history of her host nation, she regretted that her teachers hadn't prepared her to fit in to the culture she was visiting. As she wrote: "American students who travel abroad cannot be expected to transcend historical, political, social, and global systems of power in order to become cross-culturally immersed 'global citizens.' We can, however, be asked to become internationally conscious and self-aware American citizens who are responsible for thinking about those critical issues."[2]

I agree with Talya that all of us, particularly Americans, must understand how we are viewed by those around us when we visit another country. I believe many have the potential to become global citizens if we combine the abilities both to adapt our norms to those of other cultures and to adopt practices that are more effective than what we have been doing. The reasons for doing so are compelling. All businesses depend on growth in order to survive, and both population and economic growth are occurring at a far more rapid pace outside of the United States and Europe than within these countries. But to engage in business in these countries requires American and European business leaders to understand, at a minimum, and possibly even to embrace, the cultural norms of previously "foreign" people. This presents a daunting challenge to many Western business leaders. The courage to face this challenge may soon be required of any global business leader.

China and India are two countries that demand more of our attention as a result of their focus on education, their population size, and the rapid growth rates of their economies. China will change the nature of business simply based on its scale and cultural norms. Fogel points out that the Chinese are quite aware of education as the engine of growth and support higher education policies. Many people think the nation's state-owned enterprises will drag down the economy. But, there is enough strength from other sectors to support this growth, as its 8 percent per capita growth over the *past* 25 years attests. Leading analysts agree that China will continue to transform itself into a market economy. It does this by "promoting increasing autonomy in economic decisions as a lever of rapid economic growth." Fogel provides evidence that the "Chinese Communist Party and State Council are quite well aware that the successes of their growth policies have weakened the central government's control over daily life and access to information."[3] He concludes by answering the question: Who will promote liberal democracy in the next generation if the United States' share of world GDP declines from 22 percent to 14 percent and the EU 15 share slips from 21 percent to 5 percent? His answer is Asia.

My Awakening

In 1994, the first time I visited Shanghai, I walked on The Bund along the city's famous Nanjing road, which is framed by the elegant skyscrapers built in the early twentieth-century by international banking and trading companies. With the buildings at my back, I gazed out at the Huangpu River and the open pastures beyond that the locals called Pudong. As I strolled about the city, taking my own unofficial tour, I gained some insight into a culture that was struggling to identify itself. While I would often see men and women wearing the old-fashioned blue Mao caps, many others sported the latest European fashions. In the city's back alleys, bicycles still seemed to be the preferred mode of transportation to move goods to and from the local markets, but I also noticed an increasing number of clunky delivery trucks sputtering through the streets. China was evolving.

On a more recent visit to Shanghai in 2002, I saw a new land. The skyscrapers were still there, but the port and the once empty land beyond were now teeming with activity. Cars, trucks, and scooters buzzed through the crowded streets around the clock. I stayed in Pudong at the Hyatt Hotel, which was then the tallest hotel in the world; it cast its long shadow on both the nearby Pepsi Cola neon sign and the Starbucks next door. As I walked through the streets early in the morning, I gaped at the number of fashionable and expensive shops that had replaced the markets and stalls that once lined the avenues. Only an older woman's handmade broom, which she used to sweep the sidewalk in front of her home, betrayed the rural roots of the city's denizens.

China's cities are changing fast and the globe is shaking as a result. China's GDP grew 11.4 percent in 2007, topping the impressive growth rate of 11.1 percent it reported in 2006.[4] Yet, not all things may be as they appear. Many pundits question the data that the Chinese government provides, whether it concerns the number of avian flu cases or its rate of unemployment.[5] One thing is clear, however: if you visit China, companies and their employees strive to appear desirable to the eyes of a Westerner. I learned this firsthand when our market development team from Sara Lee Pacific Rim hired a consulting firm to identify all of the hosiery companies near major urban areas. This firm located and visited 51 companies before it identified the 5 companies it deemed to have the most potential to manufacture products to be sold in the Chinese domestic market.

Once we had our short list, it was time for me to visit our potential partners in person. As I was "kicking the tires" at one of these companies, I was impressed with the world-class knitting machines it had. It also seemed that the management team that came out to meet with us was quite well versed in hosiery production.

Being the curious person I am, though, when I passed the electrical box for the circuit breakers, I opened it, and I saw that it was completely empty! While this company had the machines and many other great attributes, the factory did not have any electricity. While infrastructure investments in electricity, railroads, and wastewater continue to rise at an incredible rate in China, foreign business leaders can't make assumptions; they need to know what they are buying. In order to do that, leaders need to have the courage to learn how to overcome their fears of cultural barriers in order to take advantage of the opportunities created by the interconnected economy. The lesson learned: trust, but verify the capabilities of your partners.

Opportunity Is Now

Leaders need to understand that to take their organizations global they need to move into emerging markets like China. While the economies of what we know as the "industrialized nations," such as the United States, Germany, and Japan, remain critical to any company's success, there are far more opportunities to be derived from positioning an organization's growth into emerging markets. In 2006 and 2007, 124 countries grew their economies by more than 4 percent each year.[6] Antoine van Agtmael, the fund manager who coined the term *emerging markets*, has identified 25 companies most likely to be the world's next great multinationals: "Four companies each from Brazil, Mexico, South Korea, and Taiwan; three from India; two from China; and one each from Argentina, Chile, Malaysia, and South Africa." The seismic change will create more opportunities as long as we act now. As Fareed Zakaria recently wrote: "The post-American world is naturally an unsettling prospect for Americans, but it should not be. This will not be a world defined by the decline of America but rather the rise of everyone else. It is the result of a series of positive trends that have been progressing over the last 20 years, trends that have created an international climate of unprecedented peace and prosperity."[7]

Company leaders no longer have a choice about capitalizing on the growth of these developing economies—the opportunity is now. As the authors of Accenture's study, *The Rise of the Multi-Polar World*, wrote: "To be successful, companies need to move away from the traditional U.S. and Europe-centric view of international business." New sources of opportunity, capital, and talent provide three major guiding principles for leaders who want to establish a presence in emerging markets.[8]

New Sources of Opportunity

Increased economic liberalization and openness have led to the creation of new global market opportunities. Emerging markets are evolving from their traditional role of low-cost suppliers into burgeoning consumer markets. Consider that China, with 395 million subscribers, is already the biggest market for mobile phones in the world. Mexico is the world's second-largest soft drink market.[9] Leaders cannot be blind to the opportunities such markets offer. Yet, each unique culture brings its own challenges along with the opportunities. As we discussed in Chapter 2, "Financial Realities," we can no longer afford to be merely observers of the interconnected economy: we need to become participants.

New Sources of Capital

Emerging markets are increasingly becoming a supplementary, and cheaper, source of capital. As emerging markets get wealthier and begin to develop a middle class, outward-bound investments will increase. Foreign direct investment (FDI) from emerging economies totaled $133 billion in 2005—accounting for 17 percent of global FDI. But leaders must prove to potential investors how their organizations are primed to take advantage of opportunities in emerging markets. Otherwise, they may find the doors to these new sources of capital closed. After all, with the rise of the emerging market multinational companies (EMM), there already is heated competition to attract these new sources of capital.

New Sources of Talent

Perhaps most importantly, emerging markets will be supplying the workforce of the future. When you recognize that China and India each have more workers than the numbers of workers in Europe, the United States, and Japan combined, you begin to understand that much of the present and future business talent comes from sources beyond the West. While global companies continue to look to emerging markets as sources for cheap labor, the facts are changing. These markets are now leveraging investments in education to groom higher-skilled workers to meet global demand for everything from legal services to technical support. India, for example, has been able to take advantage of its large and skilled labor force to attract high-end work from around the world. It is estimated that the nation now has about 28 percent of the world's outsourced information technology talent. Likewise, South Korea now graduates about the same number of engineering students as the United States—despite having a population one-sixth the size. Moreover, anyone who has hired a recent foreign college graduate will tell you that the ability of these students to write and reason in English surpasses the average American or British graduate's ability to do so. India is a preferred place for outsourcing, partially due to the educated English-speaking workforce. India graduates 495,000 technical graduates, nearly 2.3 million college students, and over 300,000 postgraduates every year.[10] As Figure 4.1 shows, tapping new sources of talent brings many challenges for leaders, depending on the skill level of the workforce. This fact demands that without having on-the-ground knowledge of the cultural ties that motivate those workers, leaders will be hard-pressed to compete for access to this emerging global labor pool.

One of my board colleagues is Larry Graev, president and CEO of The GlenRock Group, a merchant-banking firm. Larry successfully leveraged his extensive legal experience with an investment in Pangea3, a legal outsourcing firm with more than 100 employees based in Mumbai, India. The professionally trained attorneys in India perform the nonclient-facing service roles for litigation

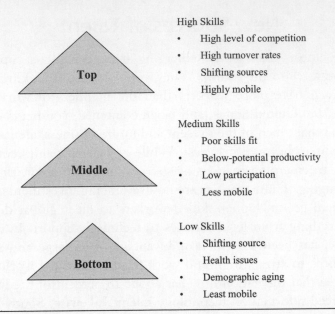

High Skills
- High level of competition
- High turnover rates
- Shifting sources
- Highly mobile

Medium Skills
- Poor skills fit
- Below-potential productivity
- Low participation
- Less mobile

Low Skills
- Shifting source
- Health issues
- Demographic aging
- Least mobile

Figure 4.1 Challenges Facing High-Performance Businesses (by Employee Skill Level) *Source:* "The Rise of the Multi-Polar World," p. 10, by Accenture, 2007.

support, document review, competitive intelligence research, routine research, and more recently, working directly with the client for a fraction of the cost of a U.S. attorney. Founded in 2004, Pangea3 has successfully demonstrated that corporations and law firms can increase their efficiency and dramatically reduce legal costs by using legal process outsourcing as a solution.

As a pioneer in the legal process outsourcing industry, Pangea3 received a significant investment from a U.S. private equity company in June 2007. The vision of Pangea3 and its investors is to enable lawyers around the globe to revolutionize the way they practice law. The amazing thing is how quickly that vision is becoming a reality. Knowing about emerging market opportunities like those tapped by Pangea3 should whet anyone's appetite for profitable growth. But the next step after identifying the opportunity is to develop your ability to work with different cultures and take action. The key is to understand the cultural nuances, allowing you to *Fit In* and work with people in your target country, as well as to *Stand Out* by bringing a mutually beneficial relationship to fruition.

Legal outsourcing is not an isolated example of professional highly skilled service jobs that now are performed outside the domestic country. Preparation of income tax returns and the analysis of x-rays for doctors are handled abroad because they can be done at least as well as in the United States, and at a considerably cheaper rate. There are several possible explanations for this phenomenon. Today's U.S. workforce may be pricing themselves out of the market, unwilling to do these jobs or, be unable to do the work due to lack of dedication or competence. At the same time, the educated talent in places like Chennai, Bangalore, Prague, Dalian, Manila, and Buenos Aires produce world-class results diligently and with positive financial returns. Productivity, not the low cost of labor, is the engine powering economic success.

Guides to the Multi-Polar World

I've learned to look for cultural guides to help me reach my business goals in different foreign countries. For example, when my boss needed to establish a sales office and center for product sourcing from China, he asked me to identify and lease the requisite office space in Hong Kong. I had never been to Hong Kong prior to this assignment. Contract terms and legal ramifications and responsibilities differ greatly in Hong Kong from the practice to which I was accustomed in the United States and Europe. Plus, many Chinese rely on the application of the ancient art of *feng shui*, the practice of arranging objects and space in a manner that helps achieve wealth, health, and personal relationship goals, before agreeing to work in a building. Being aware of auspicious locations and even that address numbers could make a difference between having a building where people will work or which people will avoid, I needed someone who understood the local market to help me. One of the first things I did was find a local real estate agent. The market in Hong Kong real estate was red hot at the time and competition for the best buildings was fierce. I worked with an agent immersed in the details and nuances of the local real estate market. Just about every day, I heard about a new company that was attempting to secure similar office spaces. Obviously, I saw the competition affecting the cost of any lease I would secure. The key was to strike a balance between a good location and labor costs to staff the business. We had to move fast: for every week we delayed to make a decision, the annual rent would rise 10 percent, changing the economics of the deal. I decided to accept any reasonable office space rather than look for an ideal one. Together, my agent and I focused on three prerequisites for any space and vowed to take the first space that met our terms. We quickly closed on the deal and leapt into the marketplace, creating a presence, which served the company well for many years.

Just as I needed to understand the intricacies of a particular real estate market in order to make an appropriate deal, the same rule applies to any individual who wants to connect with opportunities within an emerging economy. In other words, the first step to accessing new markets, sources of capital, and labor is to find a cultural guide who can explain the important nuances of that market's particular culture. The pace of decisions and change will astound you. Many individuals and their companies need to react quickly to market conditions in emerging markets or else become irrelevant. The critical skill for success in a nondomestic market is to adapt your current practices to local cultural conditions by adopting revised business goals and procedures, while still keeping your own objectives and integrity in mind. From my own experience in connecting with new markets, we can use three categories to help understand how emerging cultures differ from industrial countries in their decision making. Those categories are adopting and adapting to local customs and beliefs, role of family, and time horizons.

Adopting and Adapting to Local Customs and Beliefs

A company that wants to sell to the consumers in emerging economies such as China and India may need to change its service or product strategy to meet the local tastes. All too often, though, companies fail to adapt and, as a result, waste time and money.

Cultural mistakes can tarnish the reputation of a brand or a company, making it difficult to recover and introduce future products or services into the market. One of the most common barriers to adapting to a culture is how the new language translates concepts or words from the original language. Ford tried to sell a car called the Nova in South America when *no va* means doesn't go in Spanish. The quick-service restaurant KFC's famous slogan, "finger lickin' good," was mistranslated into Chinese as "eat your fingers off."[11] While these mistakes seem funny in hindsight, they were actually multimillion-dollar errors that could have been avoided.

Avoiding Culture Clashes

Any time your organization is headed into a new market, find someone who already knows the market, perhaps someone who emigrated from there. This is somewhat analogous to a blind person who needs a seeing-eye dog or special Braille instructions to understand what is happening. You may stumble a few times before you learn how to be effective. You may need to take the risk of appearing less competent at first in order to learn new competencies just as with any new skill. When I first moved to France, I wanted to speak as much French as possible. However, even after years of French language instruction in American schools, my skills were limited. My company hired a French woman to tutor me in the evening and I gave myself an allowance of making three language mistakes a day as encouragement to keep pushing myself to learn more. And the more I pushed myself, the more locals appreciated my efforts, even from time-to-time complimenting me when they noticed my improvements. That in turn gave me confidence and the courage to keep learning.

There are steps that Americans can take to be better prepared prior to embarking on a foreign endeavor. I suggest:

- Learn about and, if time permits, join nonprofit international affairs organizations in your area. To find a chapter near you, visit the web site of the World Affairs Councils of America at: www.worldaffairscouncils.org. The web site of the European Council on Foreign Relations has accurate material, including articles about Russia and its leadership and the many Central European emerging markets.

- Reach out to your alma mater and its alumni network. Find out if there are professors skilled in international business with whom you can talk or contact former students living in your target market.

- Read international news outlets such as the Al-Jazeera English version on the Internet or the *Economist* magazine. For a quick test of your local cultural knowledge and to see if you are headed for a culture clash in your new market, visit: www-01.ibm.com/software/globalization/clash/index.jsp.

Adapting to a local culture means more than just getting the language right—it can also mean changing your product or service offering altogether. In other words, before your product or service can stand out, you'll first need to learn how to make it fit in to the local culture.

Consider the Oreo, the chocolate-and-cream cookie made by Kraft Foods, based in Northfield, Illinois. The Oreo, introduced to Americans in 1912, has been a bestseller in the United States ever since. Kraft, like many companies in the food industry, has been stung by the rising prices of commodities like milk, wheat, and sugar, ingredients in products like Oreos. To counter that trend, Kraft, under CEO Irene Rosenfeld, has been taking advantage of the weak dollar to market products like Oreos aggressively to international markets, which now account for 40 percent of the company's total revenues. Rosenfeld has pushed more decision-making power away from corporate headquarters toward business units spread around the world. Managers in the field, who would have firsthand knowledge of the local customs and culture, have the power to shape Kraft products to suit local tastes. This strategy has led to successful new product launches such as dark chocolate bars tailored to German tastes, premium freeze-dried coffee for Russians, and special teas for Filipinos. But when it came to marketing the iconic Oreo cookie to consumers in emerging markets, Kraft had to learn how to adapt the cookie by adopting the tastes of a local culture. It now sells the classic Oreo and a special Oreo for the Chinese market.

Kraft first introduced the Oreo to China in 1996. But sales remained flat from 2000 to 2005. Worse, Kraft's rival, Nestle SA, continued to grow its market share in the $1.3 billion Chinese cookie market. Tests proved that to Chinese tastes, Oreos were too sweet. They were also too expensive. Once Kraft managers learned this important information, they did something unprecedented: they changed the Oreo. Not only did the company change things by making the cookies with less sugar, they also changed the classic round cookie into a long, thin, four-layered wafer filled with both chocolate and vanilla cream, coated in chocolate. They also put fewer cookies in a single package and dropped the price to make it more appealing to budget-conscious shoppers. Kraft continued to sell the round classic cookie in China because some of the customers wanted the Western version. Product managers ran an imaginative marketing campaign, recruiting Chinese students to ride around Beijing on bicycles with wheels that looked like the original Oreos. The campaign, which gave away cookies to some 300,000 potential customers, was a major hit and helped the Oreo to become the best-selling cookie in China. The increased sales have also made the Oreo a billion-dollar seller worldwide. The marketing efforts behind the reformulated cookie "were a stroke of genius that only could have come from local managers," Rosenfeld has said. "The more opportunity our local managers have to deal with local conditions [the more we learn about cultural nuances which] will be a source of competitive advantage for us."[12]

The story of the evolving Oreo highlights a key insight: the existence of a free market doesn't guarantee success. The market provides the parameters, but, individuals must discern ways to adapt their business to cultural nuances within those parameters. Twenty years ago, when China was still a protectionist market, consumers didn't have much choice over what kind of cookie they could eat. Even if Chinese shoppers didn't have the same kind of sweet tooth as Americans, they would have had no choice but to buy what was offered to them. But with the emergence of the interconnected economy, Chinese consumers do have choices and company leaders need to be willing to adapt to local tastes and adopt new ways to succeed. This same rule applies to tapping into new sources of capital or recruiting global workers. When it comes to understanding what motivates members of the global workforce, leaders need to understand the role of family in many cultures.

Adopting and Adapting to the Role of Family

One of the most important cultural factors is the role of family. American culture glorifies self-reliance and the decentralization of economic decisions.[13] Families have less influence on the lives of Westerners, on a daily basis, than do families in other parts of the world. I learned more about the role of family during a recent trip to India, when I met Gucharan Das, the novelist, playwright, venture capitalist, Harvard graduate, and former chief executive of Procter & Gamble in India. Das was kind enough to indulge my endless list of questions about India's evolving economy and the cultural challenges that global businesses face in integrating with local customs. Das, who has authored two books on India, explained that the nation is pluralistic.[14] With 1.2 billion people within its borders, the historic caste system, and the large number of agricultural villages and towns, India relies on the family as a stabilizing force. Das recognizes that improving the well-being of the family requires an improvement of its economic circumstances, which a free market and economic reforms can provide. "It is more important, I believe, to raise the living standards of the poor than to worry about inequality. We have to realize that economic reforms are bound to increase inequality that comes from open and free competition, but that does not mean that they will worsen the situation of the poor and the most disadvantaged."[15]

Many Indian last names will indicate where your family originated and what your religion is. Family gives an individual identity with a group and enables the many different groups to be tolerant of other groups in this pluralistic society. Compared to Western cultures, there has been less analysis and academic study about the family role in India. One study, called *The Great Indian Family* by Gitanjali Prasad, stands out. Prasad explains that the lack of work in this area results from the fact that family is so important and sacrosanct to the middle-class Indian family that no one wants to dissect and analyze it. It is as though "interrogation of the family might constitute an intrusion into that private domain where the nation's most cherished cultural values are nurtured and reproduced."[16]

Prasad writes that the family is adapting to the new forces of the workplace. In the past, the extended family of many generations living under the same roof established the cultural norms. This living arrangement faces pressure as the economy improves. With change in living arrangements comes change in social authority and personal expectation. Prasad's research shows that 20 years ago, older family members balked at younger people, particularly the women, spending so much time at work. As a result, Westerners found it hard to set the same work schedules in India as they had at home. The same is true today, but the pressure comes from a different source. Instead of a mother-in-law or husband resenting a working woman's commitment to the workplace, children do. Yet, the relationship works both ways. As they grow, there is an "overwhelming priority young people want to give their parents."[17] Westerners must adapt their expectation of workers in India to account for family dynamics. But, doing international business raises further questions that business leaders may want to consider. To what extent do businesses want to contribute to an erosion of the duties traditionally existing within Indian families? Is there a cultural trade-off that may be the basis for changes in American society?

Twenty-five or thirty years ago it was largely unheard of for an American worker in a white or blue collar job to leave work to see his son play in a high school football game. In 2008, employees routinely leave work to see their youngsters play a myriad of sports. American values, or cultural norms, have changed. What will interaction on a regular basis with people who are even more family oriented mean for American business leaders?

One example of that can be seen in career decisions. Many Indian and U.S. companies that compete for talent encourage new recruits to bring their parents to the office as part of the recruiting effort. Once the parents see the work environment, their son or daughter will be allowed to accept the offer. In India, where many young workers live with their parents, gaining parental acceptance regarding an employer and the job potential is critical given the growing shortage of workers in India's IT sector.[18] The IT consulting company Keane Inc., for example, sends recruiters to the homes of potential recruits in India to help assuage parental fears. Genpact, an Indian company that was a spin-off of General Electric, holds "Family Days" for its employees in India where parents are invited into the company's offices to get a better sense of what their children do on a daily basis. Until recently, these practices would have been unprecedented in modern industrialized cultures. But today's leaders would be remiss in not properly weighing the importance of families when it comes to recruiting, retaining, and motivating members from the global labor force.

Another clue to the impact of the family on the global labor force can be found by looking at the volume of cross-border remittance payments (see Figure 4.2).

Remittances, the portion of an immigrant worker's earnings sent home to his or her family, have been a poorly understood form of economic development for generations. Today, with an estimated 150 million migrant workers spread around the globe, the size and impact of these remittances continues to garner more and more interest from both the private and public sectors.[19] U.S. workers send an estimated $300 billion back to their families in developing countries each year, often in increments of just a few hundred dollars—adding up to about 1.5 million individual transactions each year. As Figure 4.2 shows, the bulk of remittances go to Asian emerging markets like India, which receives an estimated $24 billion each year, the most of any nation. A survey of Mexicans working in America conducted by the Inter-American Bank in 2007 found that about 75 percent of them earned less than $20,000, yet, on average, each individual sent home about $3,550 of that salary each

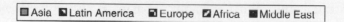

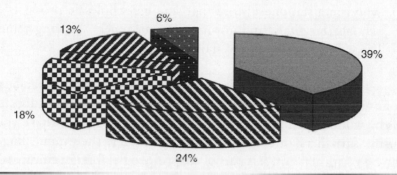

Figure 4.2 Global Remittance Distribution. *Data source*: International Fund for Agricultural Development, www.ifad.org/events/remittances/maps/.

year.[20] Another study conducted by the Migration Policy Institute in Washington, DC, found that 9,000 African doctors in America sent an average of $20,000 a year, even though some of those doctors had been away from Africa for more than 20 years.

Remittances from Close to Home

One of my regular companions is Bashir Mohamed, a native of Sudan who drives me to the airport when I leave and return from business travels. On our trips over the years, we have talked about his business. Every few months or when he manages to put aside enough money, Bashir wires money to members of his family who still live in Sudan. As an unmarried man, Bashir supports his mother, his sister, and her two children as well as his brother and his children. He has sent enough money back home to build a home for his mother. "For me, I won't take one penny with me when I die," he told me. "Life is like sitting in the shade under a tree. When the sun comes, the shade is gone. If my family is not happy, I'm not happy." Bashir is also something of an entrepreneur: he contributes to an automobile trading business where his cousin buys cars and sells them to others throughout Sudan. He also directs some of his money to family members who run a stationery store that supplies wholesale products to schools, hospitals, and government customers. Valuing family keeps Bashir working seven days a week.[21]

These figures and trends reveal how crucial family ties can be to your workforce, regardless of where your company might be located in the world. Taking the time to listen and understand where your business partners' or employees' hearts as well as their minds linger can be a critical point. It is part of adapting to the foreign cultures on which America is increasingly dependent. Knowing that one of your top engineers is sending money back to his home nation could mean you have an opportunity to help as well. Knowing the motivation and important cultural triggers that define your employee's identity gives you great insight into your employee's priorities as well as the makeup of his character.

Adopting and Adapting to Time Horizon

Another key aspect of understanding emerging markets is the context of a time horizon. In 1991, on one of my first visits to Singapore, I stayed at the Shangri La Hotel, which, at the time, was one of the island nation's newer buildings. The one thing I'll never forget was the pace of construction and renewal all around me. Workers climbed bamboo scaffolding all day and night; floodlights turned the night into day. I remember the sense of hard work the workers exhibited, toiling away at a constant pace throughout my entire stay. It was as if they were the tortoise and not the hare in a race for economic success. While others rested, they worked. To me, seeing the pace of change in Singapore was a lesson in how different cultures embrace the concept of time.

India is a nation in which change happens in a subtler manner than in Singapore. Whenever we label India simply as an emerging market, though, we fail to acknowledge the long and rich history of the nation's people and culture. India was an economic superpower in the fifteenth century and remained so until it became a colony of Great Britain.[22] China, too, was long a dominant trading power in the world and only now, after its long experiment with communism, has it begun the transition back to the principle of a free, more open market. In the twentieth century, Americans dominated the world economy and spread a culture rooted in immediate gratification. Whether it comes to reporting financial results or making investments in the education of our young, it seems that American policies are often dictated by the here and now, rather than by considering the longer term. But emerging cultures also face a struggle to catch up with industrialized countries.

In his book, *In Spite of the Gods: The Rise of Modern India*, journalist Edward Luce writes about how, in a multi-polar world, countries like India and China are not only striving to improve their own economic lot, they are also striving to mend their fences.[23] He suggests several reasons for this closer relationship. First, China is not interested in a nuclear arms race with India and investing in these nonproductive assets. "The second reason for the thawing of tensions between India and China is economic. . . . India has achieved a modest trade surplus with China [which] drastically changed Indian perceptions of China; from being a commercial threat it has become a potential partner." The increasing trade between India and China will no doubt affect the United States and its business relationships at home and abroad. The hegemony of the United States will weaken. As Luce writes, "continental shelves shift at a rate that is imperceptible to nonspecialists then one day the tectonic pressure hits a breaking point and suddenly everything that went undetected for decades becomes apparent to all."[24] This analogy illuminates how cultural norms change. To connect with India and China, global leaders need to understand the long-term diplomacy and vision of Asia's leaders. Manmohan Singh, India's prime minister said: "Together India and China can reshape the world."[25] To grasp the trends of tomorrow, leaders need to take a closer look at the kinds of decisions being made today that shape those trends—even if they might take decades to become obvious.

Media outlets in industrialized nations often imply that China is some kind of economic threat that appeared overnight. Not true. Deng Xiaoping, in 1979 was the first Chinese leader to visit the United States, meeting with President Carter in the White House. Shortly after this meeting, the United States broke diplomatic relations with the Republic of China (Taiwan) and established them with the People's Republic of China (PRC). This led many companies to fight for the removal of trade barriers between the PRC and developed countries. Although often the best laid plans for companies struggling to gain a foothold take longer to reach fruition than expected, progress has been made. A milestone was reached in 1993 with the U.S.-China market access agreement in which China pledged to eliminate many of its import quotas and other market barriers over five years.[26] In addition to working with external parties, China focuses on improving internal capabilities, at any cost. For example, China has had a long-range view toward improving its nation's infrastructure. Consider the story of the Three Gorges Dam on the Yangtze River, a $25 billion project that was planned in the early 1940s. Construction began in 1994 and should be completed in 2009. Even to begin the project, the nation tackled the logistical nightmare of moving almost two million people from villages that would eventually be submerged under a massive reservoir. Once complete, though, the 1.2-mile long dam will not only provide a key water source, its generators will increase the nation's power-generating capability by 10 percent.[27]

The Chinese have also had a long-range view of their investments in education. In 1977, for instance, as the country emerged from its Cultural Revolution, the government reinstated its nationwide university entrance exam for anyone between the ages of 13 and 37.[28] Before these exams were introduced, however, you could argue that this was a lost generation, sacrificed for the ideals of the revolution's leaders. By focusing only on fitting in—because anyone who stood out would be knocked down—this generation lost its chance for the kind of education needed to properly integrate with the requirements of the modern world. But, once the revolution ended, and more liberal thinking prevailed, the select few from that generation who had the capability to pass the exam—and the courage to raise their hand to ask for that opportunity—now have the potential to become leaders. Because their conviction was tested through years of hardship, they emerged stronger and armed with the courage to take advantage of this opportunity and to rebuild the economy. This generation is now the one that wields China's economic, political, and cultural power.[29]

As these examples indicate, China's embrace of capitalism is infused with a significant emphasis on governmental programming. *In 2007, for the first time, China contributed more to global GDP growth, at market exchange rates, than the United States.*[30] The GDP of China grew by $333 billion; the GDP of the U.S. grew by $298 billion. China also remains stable, prepared to handle domestic and global economic crises, such as U.S. economic recession, or falling stock prices. Despite a weaker banking system, China has large foreign-exchange systems in reserve, and a government with enough money to write off any bad loans.

As a direct result of its investment in education, China is graduating more engineers than any other country in the world. While the estimates vary widely, the best guesses peg the number of Chinese engineering students at more than 350,000 a year—which is more than double the number U.S. universities graduate.[31] Because of this investment, we are already seeing a shift where China will no longer just be a nation of assemblers, but of innovators. India now graduates roughly the same number of engineers as the United States does. When you combine that kind of a skilled workforce with a modernizing infrastructure, the result is a shift in the source of the world's R&D away from today's industrialized nations and to emerging markets like China, India, and Brazil.

China's traditionally strong investment in education is accelerating. "There are now some 4.2 million freshmen entering the university system annually, four times the number in the mid-1990s."[32] In addition, the Chinese are now learning business practices and management techniques from the West. An American business school consortium, led by Fordham University in New York, contributed to BiMBA, a Beijing school that launched an executive MBA program in 2000 to attract the heads of companies and their most talented employees. As the coordinator for the U.S. schools, John Yang says, "In China you are not passing on pure technical business school knowledge. The Chinese are engaging in a mental, spiritual, ideological, and psychological transformation of themselves."[33] It is easy to project that in the next decade, as the Chinese and Indian economies continue to surge, the picture of where R&D investments are made could become even more lopsided.

Snapshot of the Future

India, like China, is rapidly evolving—though in different ways. While China is often likened to agile creatures like tigers or monkeys, India is often equated to an elephant; meaning that the nation tends to move more cautiously and slowly because of the number of parties involved in making the decisions that will shape the nation's future path. Because India is a democratic state, decisions take far longer to process due to the sheer number of people that need to reach an agreement. India too relies heavily on public-private partnerships to tackle its large infrastructure projects like airports and railways.[34] This is a creative way to combine the resources of the government with some entrepreneurial know-how. But getting a project approved can take far longer than in nations with more powerful central governments like China or Japan. Unlike more developed countries, emerging markets often rely on direct government intervention in their attempt to accelerate business growth. The key for leaders is to dig into the roots of a culture to identify who the main decision makers are. Tear back the curtain to learn who drives the ultimate decision: the leaders from the company, the government, or a public-private partnership. Your opportunity to serve the market and its people will depend on this analysis.

Key Points to Consider

- What kinds of cultural biases do you or your team members operate under? If you change your lens, are there new opportunities for you to explore outside your current comfort zone?

- When was your last trip outside your home country? Perhaps it's time to take an exploratory trip to India, China, or another emerging market.

- If you are already operating in international markets, are there additional local partners to engage in order to accelerate and deepen your integration with the local culture and economy?

- Consider the demographic shifts in your home country. What can you do to prepare yourself better to tap into the global workforce?

- What does your long-term strategic forecast look like? Is there room for you to think about how the world's shifting cultural norms could impact your organization's long-term strategy?

The Next Stop

Now that we have taken the time to understand how to adopt and adapt to three critical categories of cultural norms that drive the workings of emerging markets, our next stop will be to understand how critical today's youth are to success in the interconnected economy—as well as how leaders can better engage with and connect with the members of Gen Y.

CHAPTER
5

Winning the Battle
for Talent

As we complete the first decade of the twenty-first century, most of the risks and opportunities from the globalization of business are not as predictable as the demographics we face in the workforce. Youths entering the workforce were born 25 to 30 years ago to replace the aging workforce. However, *where* the employees are located will create a major disruption of past economic centers and shift in economic vibrancy between countries and parts of the world. Leaders of organizations based in developed economies face a mounting challenge: the aging of their workforces. Some estimates predict that 500 of the biggest companies in the United States could lose half their senior managers to retirement over the next five years, with certain industries particularly hard hit.[1] In the U.S. energy sector, for example, more than 33 percent of the workforce is age 50 or older, while the aerospace industry has a workforce that is 40 percent over age 50. Japan is already beginning to feel the effects of its rapidly aging population. The number of workers over the age of 50 employed in the Japanese financial services sector is expected to grow to 61 percent by the year 2020.[2] While current workers are expected to remain employed longer than those of past generations, most experts still predict potential talent shortages in Japan and Western European countries as their older workers begin to retire.

As retirement stretches further into the future for some workers and a new generation of young employees enters the workforce, the corporate world finds 60-year-olds working side-by-side with recent college graduates. In order to work effectively with four generations in the workforce, leaders must recognize and understand how each group communicates.

Traditionalists, Baby Boomers, Gen X, and Gen Y are some of the labels researchers and marketers apply to people of different age groups that compose today's global workforce. These classifications are similar across the United States, Europe, and Australia. But even China experienced three baby booms in the early 1950s, 1960s, and late 1980s. In 1973, at the time the Chinese politicians instituted the policy of one child per family, the birth rate was 5.8 children per family.[3] Rural couples have been allowed to have a second child if the first was a girl since 1984, creating another baby boom. This generation has grown up in parallel with children born after 1980 in the Western world and been exposed to many of the same life events, like the fall of the Berlin Wall, creating their assumptions about the world, many of which form during the teenage years.

Research shows that each generation has unique motivations and beliefs. Courageous leadership, therefore, requires understanding how a business might integrate people of different generations. Many leaders act as if what was good for their generation is good for the next generation. They may not understand the world has changed. People of different ages are motivated differently, often as a result of political events or social movements occurring in their adolescent formative years. The four generations comprising today's U.S. workforce can be described as follows:

1. *Traditionals:* This generation, also known as "silents," consists of people born before 1946. The Great Depression and World War II shaped this generation's values. As employees, these

individuals value loyalty, hierarchy, and respect. They generally have good teamwork, collaboration, and interpersonal communication skills.

2. *Baby Boomers:* Some 82 million Baby Boomers were born between 1946 and 1964, joining the workforce at a time when European countries were recovering from World War II and a new prosperous era for Europe and the United States began. The Civil Rights Movement, the Vietnam experience, and the rise of the "Me Generation" culture shaped the Baby Boomer mindset. "Growing up amid these events caused many Boomers (no longer called "baby") to conclude that this was a world that was not working well, a world that needed to change."[4] One of the results of those experiences is that Boomers have a strong drive to succeed. This is the first generation to declare a higher priority for political and personal aspects of life than for their jobs.

3. *Generation X:* A generation born between 1965 and 1980 with advanced academic training and, often with some exposure to international travel, this group breaks traditional patterns of behavior. The 40 million members of this generation often demand a more informal environment and value horizontal structures over hierarchy. Personal initiative is evident in the many entrepreneurial ventures begun by members of this generation and at large companies that harness their Gen Xers' motivation.

4. *Generation Y:* This group, born after 1980 consists of approximately 70 to 75 million new workers in the United States.[5] These young members of what people have begun to call Gen Y or the "Millennial generation" grew up surrounded by technology and cannot imagine life without this advantage. This group is proud to be identified as Gen Y, eager to hear about themselves and may be considered a "tribe." Many of the members of this group also enjoyed comfortable and prosperous youths, which has fostered many individuals who value personal activities above social and labor considerations. Individuals are less

likely to respond to traditional command-and-control working methods. This group tends to change jobs frequently, often every one to three years. This group not only represents American youth, it also defines most of the global workforce. In other words, this is the generation with the potential to shake the globe. By sheer numbers and ability to use technology, Gen Y sets many of today's trends and seeks foreign experiences.

One of the more interesting aspects of Gen Y is that members of this generation, more than any other, share similar attributes regardless of their country of origin. The primary reason for this interconnectedness is technology like the Internet that enables today's youth to think of themselves as global citizens. The clear opportunity for companies and organizations is to use communication tools like the Internet to connect with young people—no matter where they live. As *Wall Street Journal* columnist Carol Hymowitz wrote:

> *Executives seeking to expand their companies' global reach long have focused on tailoring products to fit the local tastes of consumers in different countries. Increasingly, however, they also have a strong sense of the commonality of their global consumers. As the world shrinks, especially for young, Internet-savvy consumers, they must now also cater to particular subcultures of customers who share very similar outlooks, styles and aspirations despite their different nationalities and languages.*[6]

Similar generation attitude groupings exist around the world. As Table 5.1 demonstrates, it is the populations in developed nations that are aging; the workforce of the future is clearly going to originate within the emerging markets. It is there that the battle for talent will be waged. There are an estimated 3.5 billion people under the age of 30 in the world as of 2007—including 1.7 billion between the ages of 15 to 29—most of whom reside in developing nations (Figure 5.1).

Table 5.1 World Population: Developed versus Developing Nations

	2007 Population (in millions)	Less than Age 15 (%)	Greater than Age 65 (%)	Projected Population Growth Rate, 2007–2050 (%)
Developed nations	1,221	17	16	3
Developing nations	5,404	31	6	49
World	6,625	28	7	40

Source: *2007 World Population Data Sheet*, Washington, DC: Population Reference Bureau, 2007.

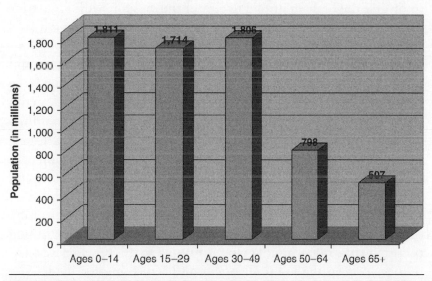

Figure 5.1 World Population by Age. *Data source:* U.S. Census Bureau, www.census.gov.

Today's Workforce

The solution to avoiding the crisis of a shortage of talented workers in the right markets requires that today's leaders need to connect with today's youth—those young workers born after 1980 who have been branded with the label Generation Y (Gen Y). Members of Gen Y are more globally attuned than those of earlier generations and thus could potentially transform the organizations competing in the interconnected economy. The dilemma for most organizations is that demand for young talent has become increasingly fierce as many nations around the world begin to feel the pinch of their aging populations. Developing nations have increasing needs for young workers as its current workforce ages and retires, exacerbating the need for talented workers close to home. As the authors of Accenture's report wrote: "Indigenous companies are looking to keep the most valuable individuals and are being aided by governments keen to reverse the brain drain and to attract the diaspora workforce back into the domestic labor market."[7] For example, Mexico has initiated a program that enables young workers to communicate through radio programs, magazines, and the Internet with government and private enterprises. Argentina has a similar initiative called the National Program on Youth Inclusion which aims to promote activities that encourage young workers to seek employment within the country's borders rather than migrating to seek other opportunities.[8] Indonesia, the Republic of Korea, and Senegal have also begun programs to create jobs for its young people, including funding several micro-enterprise startups.

Finding the means to focus today's youth can involve separating the new workforce from existing older workers. That means focusing on productive opportunities close to home that leverage new technology to keep the job challenging and intriguing for them. The tension between too much technology for the older group and not enough for the younger group creates a working dynamic that has two different paces of work. The older boss might think an analysis will take three weeks, when the younger worker can often write an automated routine for a computer program called a macro to have the work done in a day or less. This generation gap also creates new recruiting and retention challenges for global organizations. The term *generation gap* first came into prominence in the 1960s and was used to describe the cultural differences between the Baby Boomers and their parents.[9] Today's gap, on the other hand, applies more to the age difference that exists between seasoned business leaders and their younger workers. Not only do younger workers today tend to be far more tech-savvy than their parents, they also grew up in an environment that taught them to question their leaders. Overcoming these challenges and successfully tapping the global talent pipeline requires learning how to eliminate the "new generation gap" with today's youth around the globe and focus them on delivering economic value to the organization. Leaders, many of whom view assumptions about work and life through the lens or perspective of a Boomer as they moved through their careers, need to acquire the ability to cast off any bias they may have formed from working in traditional business environments. If you were to travel to São Paulo, Brazil, for example, you would notice the young people wear t-shirts, not suits or ties, to their office jobs. But appearances can be deceiving. Regardless of their dress, this next generation is tech-savvy, open-minded, and unresponsive to the command-and-control way of leading. People of the younger generation communicate through different networks from prior generations. As the authors of consultancy Deloitte's 2007 IMPACT survey of Gen Y wrote, "Between their fast-paced upbringing and their exposure to a culture in which philanthropy is growing in importance, Gen Y is a new breed, and one with the drive, confidence and skill to become the most socially focused and entrepreneurial generation to date."[10] If leaders want to access some of this talent pool, they may need to look beyond the differences in personal style.

The Global Generation

Researchers have begun calling the Gen Y workforce the *global generation*. Professor Boris Porkovich, an associate dean at the

International University of Monaco, has argued that business schools around the world are facing a new challenge: how to maximize the potential of the next generation of business leaders. Porkovich's research indicates that geography, culture, and communication are now so interwoven into the very life fabric of today's business leaders that they are, in effect, a "global generation." "Freed from the shackles of an outdated internationalist view, this generation's members are inextricably linked to each other and the new reality of a universal noncomfort zone."[11]

The intense competition for talent in our interconnected globe means that leaders need to be able to connect with this generation's top performers—no matter what country that individual calls home. The Washington, DC-based Pew Research Center for the People and the Press conducted a survey of some 66,000 people in 49 different countries. Those participating in the survey were asked the question: "How do you feel about the world becoming more connected through greater economic trade and faster communications?" Table 5.2 shows the percentage of respondents who responded to the question with an answer of "very good."

Table 5.2   Support for Globalization: Youth Has Positive View about Connecting through Economic Trade

| Area | Ages | | | |
	18–29 (%)	30–49 (%)	50–64 (%)	65+ (%)
North America	43	35	35	27
Western Europe	41	37	40	36
Eastern Europe	39	30	30	7
Latin America	36	36	44	45
West Africa	75	66	58	61
East/South Africa	59	51	48	31
Conflict Area*	50	50	45	39

*Countries include Egypt, Jordan, Lebanon, Pakistan, Turkey, and Uzbekistan.
Source: "A Global Generation Gap: Adapting to a New World," Washington, DC: Pew Research Center, February 24, 2004, http://people-press.org/commentary/display.php3?AnalysisID=86 (accessed August 30, 2008).

As the results in Table 5.2 demonstrate, except for those in Latin America, today's young people—those under the age of 30—are the most receptive to the idea of operating in an interconnected world. While the study fails to answer why young Latin Americans lag behind their global peers nor does it include Asians, the message remains clear: today's youth are embracing the interconnected world. Assuming that they receive an adequate education and develop requisite skills, this is good news for companies that seek the best and brightest beyond their local markets. There is a battle for talent, with companies all over the globe trying to reconfigure their organizations to become more attractive to the most talented members of this burgeoning generation. Knowing how to connect and engage with Gen Y employees will separate successful multinational companies from those that struggle and fail.

Connecting and Engaging

The challenge for leaders is how to both connect and engage with members of this generation while continuing to develop the existing workforce composed of workers from earlier generations. Members of Gen Y in the United States, for example, require more positive feedback than previous generations. The worldwide public accounting firm KPMG provides its senior management with thank-you note cards with iTunes, Starbucks, and gift cards from other shopping destinations popular with Gen Y to give to the staff in their twenties to recognize their hard work during the busiest season of year-end auditing. KPMG understands that, to grow its business, it must engage its younger workers. KPMG excels at engaging today's youth because it vigorously and continuously takes action to do so and promotes its values through its people and through its web site, which has a section called *Why and How People Flourish at KPMG*.

One of the rules-of-thumb when interviewing and hiring younger workers is that while they may have high self-esteem, they also suffer from a lack of confidence. Self-esteem reflects a person's general sense of self-worth. Confidence reflects self-esteem coupled with beliefs about capabilities to accomplish specific tasks and likelihood of succeeding. Recognize that, in the United States at least, many parents raised their Gen Y children with the expectation that they were special and would always be loved. As a result, this is a generation that receives a trophy for trying. Teachers will often bestow an award on an entire class rather than singling out the true winner in a competition. Recent studies, however, reveal that confidence can only be attained through the achievement of real goals and by succeeding in trials evaluated with true standards, not wishful thinking. Leaders from this generation can only be cultivated if they move out of their comfort zone, by testing themselves and developing confidence by tackling projects of all sizes. Only then can a leader develop the authentic characteristics to succeed in this global world.

Leaders need to force Gen Y workers out of their comfort zone. Recent scientific research exploring the brain stimulus and connection with happiness shows that "satisfaction comes less from the attainment of a goal and more in what you must do to get there."[12] Gregory Berns, an associate professor of psychiatry and behavioral sciences at Emory University, examined the effects of physical and mental activity on gaining confidence and satisfaction. His research is compelling in proving that being tested and receiving feedback leads to a healthy development of the psyche.

I recently encountered another example of the challenge of connecting with younger workers when I questioned an employee at Pepsi Bottling Group about how her search was going for a new strategy person. As a fellow Boomer, she confessed that many of the resumes of today's young people look very different than those we used to interview for our early jobs. She pointed out that one candidate who worked for a top consulting firm and had great experience, clearly had the strategic ability, intelligence, and the engaging personality to be a courageous leader. Yet, on her resume she had included her high school SAT scores along with a bullet point that stressed her fondness for dancing and funky music. Not only did this candidate apparently think this information was relevant and important, she also was bold enough to ask in her interview,

"What do you think about rehiring me if I leave in two years to go get an MBA?" Before she had even been hired, she was already talking about leaving the company. Her concern was for what the company would do for her, not for how she could serve the company's needs. The challenge is how to overcome the paradox at the core of this generation: How do you connect with individuals who don't respond to the traditional model of leadership that relied on command and control? The answer begins with leaders embracing the role of technology.

Communicating through Technology

The secret to tapping into technology and using it to communicate your message is to provide customization. Today's youth want to be part of a subculture, but also to stand apart as special. Understanding technology is, in many ways, the key to connecting with a country's youth. The catch for courageous leaders, therefore, is to learn the nuances of how to connect with the youth who are the products of their own unique cultures. As an example, Procter & Gamble is using the Internet both to conduct market research and to provide information on its products in its feminine-care line through a single web site that is translated into 40 languages. "We're seeing global tribes forming around the world that are more and more interconnected through technology," says Melanie Healey, president, Global Health and Feminine Care at Procter & Gamble, Cincinnati.

These global tribes tend to congregate around similar interests. An example of this was the dawn of the MTV revolution. Music has always been an element that could tie together or divide subcultures, young people in particular. With MTV, music took on a new dimension in addition to sound: you could see the musicians perform and emulate styles. And today music is as popular as ever—it seems iPod ear buds are ubiquitous no matter where you travel. In addition to watching MTV, young people today turn to the Internet and web sites like MySpace or YouTube to check out videos and live performances of their favorite bands around the world. It is not only music that connects today's youth—it is also video games, comic books, and sports. More significantly, the Internet, specifically the evolving dimension of online collaboration, is enabling young people with similar interests to connect all around the globe. As Sarah Perez, a writer who covers the Gen Y crowd, describes it: "The term 'digital native' applies to most Gen Y'ers. Those in Gen Y grew up around computers, the Internet, mobile phones, video games and mp3 players. They are web savvy multitaskers, able to watch TV, surf the web, listen to music, and talk or text on their phones, often performing several of these things at the same time."[13]

The key for today's leaders, therefore, is to understand the critical component in reaching out to members of this generation: social media.

Web 2.0 Changes Everything

The Internet's first boom in popularity started in the 1990s with the introduction of the Mosaic browser, later to become Netscape, that brought together information and images from around the globe. The so-called "killer app" for Internet users, however, was e-mail: the ability for people to communicate across vast distances at virtually no cost. While the amount of information and data on the Internet continues to expand, recent changes in the underlying technology comprising the Web's backbone—the dawn of Web 2.0—created the current wave of popularity that has so engrossed Gen Y. Simply defined, Web 2.0 is the evolution of the Internet from a one-way broadcast mechanism to a sophisticated platform for collaboration. Web 2.0 includes new tools like blogs, wikis, and file sharing of everything from photos to video.[14] The most well-known example of which is *Wikipedia*, the online user-generated encyclopedia. With these tools, users have transformed the Internet from simply a broadcast mechanism to a nest of collaboration.

It is the social media web sites in particular to which leaders need to pay close attention. These sites collectively have become the face of Web 2.0, which in turn has become the connective glue for Gen Y not only in the United States but around the world. Young people spend an increasing percentage of their day either updating their own home page or trolling through their friends' sites to find the latest scoop. Endless webs of pictures, diaries, and digital music collections abound. A study done by research firm Forrester found that 24 percent of members of Gen Y read blogs, which is twice as many as Gen Xers and three times the number of Baby Boomers.[15] A study conducted by research firm Synovate found that young Asians in countries like Malaysia, Thailand, and Hong Kong spent up to 12 hours a day either online or using their mobile phones.[16] Social media have become the virtual connection for youth and a rapidly growing percentage of the entire global generation.

For instance, Facebook, a social networking site that connects people with their friends, family, and just about anyone else, was founded by 20-year-old Mark Zuckerberg out of his Harvard dorm room. Facebook expanded globally in the first year of its existence, enrolling students throughout the United States, Canada, Mexico, the United Kingdom, Australia, New Zealand, and Ireland. In fact, some 60 percent of its estimated 70 million users come from outside the United States. Facebook isn't creating separate sites for distinct countries; users have the ability to flip a virtual switch to translate the entire site into languages like Spanish, German, or French. MySpace, the largest social network with a reported 114 million users, is also recruiting members in countries like Russia, Turkey, Poland, and Portugal and now, about 45 percent of its users come from outside the United States—an increase of roughly 30 percent from 2006.[17] Friendster, one of the early pioneer social media sites in the Web 2.0 movement, has been largely ignored in the United States, but has become the network of choice for young people in the Philippines. Other fast-growing sites include Yaari, Hi5, Google-owned Orkut, and Bebo, which AOL purchased for a reported $1 billion in early 2008.[18]

There has been an explosion in the number of social networking clones and competitors around the world since MySpace and Facebook have come to prominence. The list of imitation sites includes Europe's StudiVZ, Mixi in Japan, Australia's studentface.com.au, China's xiaonei.com, and Russia's vkontakte.ru. More social network users already exist in Asian and Europe than in North America, while the fastest growth in terms of adding new users is coming from the

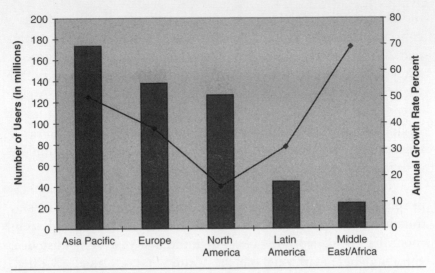

Figure 5.2   Global Social Networking Usage. *Data source:* Jon Swartz, "Social-Networking Sites Going Global," *USA Today*, February 2008.

Middle East and Africa (Figure 5.2). "Literally hundreds of millions of people around the world are visiting social networking sites each month and many are doing so on a daily basis," said Bob Ivins, the executive vice president for international markets at ComScore, the international Web monitoring agency. "It would appear that social networking is not a fad but rather an activity that is being woven into the very fabric of the global Internet."[19]

Embracing the Network

For leaders waging the battle for talent, understanding the critical role social networks play in the lives of Gen Y recruits is critical. While these networks often serve as repositories for vast stores of personal information, their members also use them as sounding boards. Before responding to a job posting, for example, a Gen Yer might send out a message to his or her social network to find out more about your company—or to ask if someone even better might be hiring. Job-hunting web sites like CareerBuilder, Jobster, and Yahoo! HotJobs are already building connection points to

Facebook.[20] Sites like Facebook "are a great medium for employers to become more relatable to this important segment of the workforce," says Richard Castellini, vice president of consumer marketing at CareerBuilder.[21] Chris Russell founded his job-hunting site, JobsinPods.com, using podcasts, digital sound files that are another of the new Web 2.0 tools. Rather than just post a text-based job ad, companies can now record a podcast about the career opportunities within their organization. "The iPod generation is bored with conventional communication techniques that employers use to reach them," Mr. Russell says. "They want something fresh and real, like podcasts, which are very commonly used within this group."[22]

Survey results published by Universal McCann show that social media have a strong impact on an organization's reputation; 36 percent of the 17,000 users from 29 countries who responded said that they thought more positively about a company that has a blog.[23] Modern organizations need to be extremely aware of what type of material about the company is already online. If something bad has been written, a simple Google search will likely reveal it.

Gen Yers will also expect to have access to collaborative tools in the workplace. Why shouldn't they tap their personal network for sales leads or possibly some tips on solving an information technology (IT) headache? The same tools can be used to link the members of an organization effectively as well. "Younger workers don't just want social-networking style tools such as instant messaging, Facebook, wikis, blogs, and so on—they expect them," writes Sarah Perez.[24] Rather than resist these impulses, savvy leaders make these tools available. An extra step some companies take to lure and engage Gen Yers is to subsidize text-messaging plans for individuals' cell phones or provide a wireless networking card for their laptops at home. Global companies like Ernst & Young, as one example, is already using video blogging to provide an "intern's eye's view" to recruit prospective recruits. Again, the key for leaders is to transform their organizations in order to become better recruiters of global talent. "The upcoming generation is going to have a major impact on business. She will expect to have access to her tools in the workplace," said Marthin De Beer, a senior vice president with

Cisco Systems. "Web 2.0 empowers users beyond creating content. It's about how we interact. For the next generation, it will be about mass collaboration, using social networking."[25]

At the same time, granting access to tools like blogs and social networks at work brings risks as well. Leaders must learn, just as they did when the Internet and e-mail first made it into the office, to coach their younger workers that just because they give complete access to their personal lives via their daily blog, there is some information about the workplace that is not for public consumption. According to experts, some of the challenges of introducing social media into the workplace include:[26]

- *Decreased productivity:* What happens when workers of any generation begin using their new social media tools more for socializing than for forming intercompany links or securing sales leads? Leaders will need to come up with appropriate rules of use or perhaps even employ monitoring tools.

- *Jeopardized security:* Introducing social media tools requires a team effort with an organization's IT department to ensure the organization's information is securely locked down from outside access. Team members must also be briefed as to what information should be off-limits for any external discussion.

- *Predefined rules:* Leaders need to sit down with their team members and set up predefined rules of use that will apply to how social media tools should be used as part of their job. The same rule applies to young job seekers who expose too much information on their MySpace page: they have unintentionally shared too much information (about significant others, parties attended, risky pictures, etc.) with potential employers or, worse, shared information about the job to competitors. Using collaborative tools to reveal personal information for all the public to view could lead to gossip, rumors, grudges, and even sexual harassment. Team members must be taught that the organization's reputation is at stake and they are representing the organization. By establishing rules about what can or should be said, leaders can prevent misunderstandings down the road.

The goal for leaders of any age, therefore, is to initiate an open dialog with younger, more tech-savvy team members in order to access their thoughts and ideas about how best to leverage social media tools and then to establish rules that will both benefit and secure the organization.

Social Media 101

Your organization wants to tap into the social media network, but where do you start? With new web sites, blogs, and networks emerging overnight in countries all over the world, it can be difficult to get a firm grip on where your organization should be making investments in time and research. One place to begin your education is a relatively new social media resource introduced by a partnership of two global media companies called the Social Media Portal which can be accessed at www.socialmediaportal.com.[27]

This tool creates a virtual map that allows users to select from different social media such as social networks, virtual communities, or blogs and then drill down into different countries to find out what the dominant player is in that geographical region. This tool allows you to easily identify the most popular social networks in Russia and China or find out what the most popular online gaming community is in Brazil.

Intimate, Yet Isolated

The reliance of today's youth on technology and social media does have at least one downside: it creates a paradox of intimacy. While young people share every detail about their lives on their social networking page or can endlessly chat or text message on their mobile phones, they do so in a "virtual" environment without any actual physical interaction with other human beings. I am reminded of a story a Hollywood executive recently told me. He was driving his daughter and two of her friends home from school when the young girls' conversation in the back seat turned to descriptions of the good looks of Orlando Bloom, star of the movies *Pirates of the Caribbean* and *Lord of the Rings*. My friend had worked with Mr. Bloom, and chimed in on the conversation, adding how nice a guy Mr. Bloom was. Catching his daughter's eyes in the rearview mirror though, he received a look that clearly said, "Dad, please be quiet." After a few more minutes, he noticed that all was quiet in the back seat. Looking back, he saw his daughter, seated in the middle, texting away on her cell phone. "Honey," he said. "Don't be rude and play with your phone while you're sitting next to your friends." This time, his daughter fixed him with an even sterner look before replying that she was actually sending these very friends text messages so that he couldn't hear what they were saying. Today's youth will find ways to communicate and socialize using a new definition of etiquette.

Mobile phones in particular have become the de facto means of communication for more than just young girls in California. Japanese young people are such fanatical cell-phone users that they have created a subculture of literature by typing out novels on their phones' tiny keyboards. One 21-year-old woman named Rin penned a novel titled *If You* over a six-month stretch during her senior year of high school. After she uploaded "the novel" to a popular web site, it gained widespread attention. A major publisher chose to publish the work, eventually selling 400,000 copies—making it the fifth best-selling novel in Japan for 2007.[28] This story is likely just the beginning, as "next generation" mobile phones like Apple's iPhone begin to play an increasing role in the everyday lives of Gen Y. Tech guru Lee Gomes forecasts a further explosion in the use of these so-called "smart" phones. "People are continuing to migrate to new uses on their phones, making them computers on their hips," he wrote. "It's not just voice, of course. They are e-mailing with them, and watching TV. People are even starting to record video programs on their phones, like they were living-room digital video recorders."[29]

While these new potential uses of technology are exciting, they also pose a challenge for leaders, namely how do you connect with people who might not even look up from the screen in front of his or her face? A similar problem is that while communication technology like Internet-based telephony and video conferencing has made it easier to work from anywhere in the world, the only interaction between team members winds up being "virtual." Virtual workers work physically separate from their bosses, colleagues, or direct reports. While there are many advantages to enabling such work environments, the downside is learning how to adapt and engage these "virtual" workers. In fact, the temptation may be to allow employees to take the easy and nearby assignments. The result, though, is that these employees could lose out on developmental opportunities in a new physical location, whether it is within the home country or on an international assignment. "Nothing can replace face-to-face communication," says Christine Communal, a senior researcher at Cranfield University's Center for Research into the Management of Expatriation. "If you do hit problems, the risk is that you haven't had time to properly build up a relationship with your local employees to help you work them out."[30] To solve the problems resulting from isolation created by Web 2.0, a good face-to-face conversation in the office or in an off-site meeting must happen more frequently than it does now. When building collaboration and communication skills with others, nothing can substitute for breathing the same air and breaking bread with another person.

Inspiring a Cause

One of the key motivators for many of Gen Y members is working with socially responsible companies that make a positive difference in the world. This suggests that your organization needs to be thinking about its role in the world if you want to attract talented workers. According to Evan Hochberg, national director of community involvement for Deloitte: "Companies with strong outward-facing community involvement programs have a leg-up in the ongoing battle for Gen Y talent. Gen Y recruits want to be empowered not only to climb the corporate ladder, but also to make a meaningful difference in their communities along the way. Companies need to recognize that community involvement is a powerful proxy for helping Gen Yers understand what its vision and values are. They will look at companies that are committed, engaged and doing meaningful things and they will believe that this is a place they want to work."[31]

The Big Four accounting firms—Deloitte & Touche, KPMG, PricewaterhouseCoopers, and Ernst & Young—use a pyramid model of organization. Younger, less-experienced accountants, from recent college graduates to young professionals around age 30, perform much of the routine auditing tasks. In a pyramid model, it is essential to hire and train many new college graduates because the firms expect 50 percent of them will have left within five years. Community outreach programs can contribute to good financial results. For example, annual global revenues increased by 17 percent for Deloitte Touche to $27 billion; KPMG also reported a 17 percent increase to $20 billion in their most recent fiscal year. Yet, when economic conditions tighten, employees shift their attention from community efforts to being more motivated by parochial concerns. One of the socially responsible efforts that has spread like wildfire across the globe is to promote environmental concerns and "go green." In fact, having the reputation of supporting this cause has proven to be a powerful recruitment and retention tool. The marketing research firm Ipsos Mori found 80 percent of respondents to a broad survey conducted in 2006 across 15 developed nations "would prefer working for a company that has a good reputation for environmental responsibility."[32] The figure was 81 percent in the United States. The marketing research surveys continued country by country. In Britain, research showed that at the peak in January 2007, "19 percent of people, unprompted, named the environment as one of the biggest issues facing Britain today, compared with just a few percent several years earlier. But by January 2008, that figure had fallen to 8 percent, while the economy was rated a top concern by one in five."[33] This decline in priority for the environment reflects the more immediate concern of keeping a job and household purchasing power as people struggle with an economy reflecting the housing and banking crises and higher costs of fuel, among other uncertainties.

Some Gen Yers are choosing to take an active role in their community during their personal time or are inventing their own organizations. This practice is exemplified by the rising number of so-called "social entrepreneurs"—young people, who like the civil rights workers and antiwar protesters of the 1960s, have prioritized making contributions to society over making six- and seven-figure salaries on Wall Street. With parents willing to fund their lifestyle and interests, Gen Yers resist a paid position, preferring to work in philanthropy.

Consider the story of Andrew Klaber. After taking a hiatus from his studies at Harvard Business School, he founded the organization Orphans Against AIDS—which pays school-related expenses for children living in developing nations who have been orphaned or affected in some way by AIDS. Or consider Jennifer Staple, a former classmate of Klaber, who formed the group Unite for Sight that collects unused reading glasses in the United States and then forwards them along to some 200,000 residents of developing nations.[34] It's not just American youth creating nonprofit organizations. For example, Cheryl Perera is a 22-year-old Canadian who founded OneChild, an activist group with the objective of combating the global sex trade.[35] Bernise Ang, another 22-year-old, founded Syinc, formerly known as the Singapore International Youth Council, which helps young Singaporeans connect with social causes that inspire them. Ang explains, "Syinc is filling a niche as a catalyst for change through young people, who are smart and leverage business thinking with Web 2.0 technology such as social networking for social change."[36] The key for leaders, therefore, is to rethink how your organization is involved in the community. By organizing volunteer programs or environmental advocacy, your organization will attract potential employees or at least, avoid alienating them.

"Doing good" does not mean abandoning the principles of the free market. Soraya Salti from Jordan, for instance, founded an organization called Injaz that teaches about one million students, including many young women, in 12 Arab nations about the power of entrepreneurship to bring about social changes. (The power of global entrepreneurship is addressed in Chapter 8.) Salti provides advice for any global organization: "If you capture the youth and change the way they think, then you can change the future."[37]

Key Points to Consider

- Appearances can be deceiving. Tap into identities to find and encourage the individual's leadership potential. Do you have human facilitators to supplement independent or online training for skills required in a global economy?

- Social networks create fragmentation yet offer an opportunity for companies to use segmentation to reach their target audiences. How do you segment and reach your Gen Y customers?

- Establish clear guidelines regarding what information must remain confidential within your organization. Expect Gen Y employees to blog. So, enforce your rules to respect privacy in your global business.

- To build a thriving business, you must connect with younger workers. To do so, follow the Rule of 3 Rs: Recognize their individual "specialness." Reward them frequently. Redefine what loyalty means.

- Think about three of your major achievements. How did each build confidence and shape your courage when working in global environments?

The Next Stop

Unleashing the power of today's youth will be a challenge. Many highly skilled members of Gen Y will be able to pick and choose from options so connecting with them is essential. Our next stop will be to understand another demographic group with latent power—women—and how their evolving role is shaking the globe.

CHAPTER

6

Women Working

Women hold up half the sky.

—Chinese proverb[1]

I have spent much of my career helping women to overcome cultural and self-imposed limitations in order to find fulfillment in business. Today, I am troubled by friends and colleagues who oppose globalization because of the potential deleterious effects it may have on women's rights. Nobody can be blind to the discrimination women encounter in education and employment in many cultures throughout the world. But, I believe that globalization can help to combat this discrimination and that progress in recognizing women's rights can be made while still being open to and accepting of cultural differences.

As the authors of the 2008 "Global Employment Trends for Women" wrote: "Decent work for women is also a precondition for economic development since, in the long run, economies cannot afford to ignore an untapped resource such as that which could be offered by female labour."[2] Courageous leaders need to understand, both for the welfare of their businesses and the future of human rights in our world, the complex global landscape related to gender roles.

I recognize the privileges I enjoy with my economic and educational status compared to the situation in which I find many working women of other nations. When meeting and working with talented women in both developed as well as emerging markets, I see only a small fraction of any nation's population of women. Many may not be allowed to work for pay, or if they are, do so at low wages in difficult working conditions with little support from the political system. Clearly, many organizations do not consider the loss of women's talent in the workplace to be an issue. Yet, as organizations extend their reach in this interconnected world, the hidden and unused talent of women may be a decisive factor in raising standards of living in countries that welcome economic progress but do not want changes in their cultural status quo.

Many advocates of women's rights say that boycotts may be more effective than complicity in promoting full economic and political rights to women and other minority groups. I disagree. I believe social changes will be an outcome of the benefits of the expanded marketplace. The ideology behind free markets is rooted in an appreciation of each individual, man or woman, as a free, rational, reasonable, and independent decision maker, operating out of perceived self-interest in making economic choices. Market opportunities will encourage a greater acceptance of the ideology that underlies them. Cultural changes cannot be imposed by U.S. businesses or by laws from the U.S. government. But, if market laws are truly universal, their acceptance should lead to a growing acceptance of their underlying premises. I have full confidence that the opening of markets through free enterprise will provide radical changes in the rights of women.

In many countries, societal values teach women to stay at home and take care of the family. Women who seek employment outside of their homes are often forced to work in menial jobs and generally receive lower wages than men. However, the market demand for employees is encouraging even societies that reflect such values to educate women, allowing them to acquire skills that are highly desirable and command higher wages. Contributing to this initiative, the international community, led by UNESCO, committed itself, through the Dakar Framework for Action, to eliminate gender disparities in primary and secondary education by 2005 and to create gender equality of access to education by 2015. By learning simple computer skills, or even by learning basic nursing or caretaking techniques, for example, a woman who might otherwise work for little or no pay in agriculture could find higher paying work. More education often also means more mobility: the more skills a woman can acquire, the more freedom she has to pursue new opportunities away from her hometown. However, not all developed economies have embraced women as equal to men in the workplace.

I often use the story of a young Dutch female attorney I met in Paris in 1993 to paint a picture of this dynamic. When I asked my colleague why she chose to work in Paris as opposed to living closer to home, she patiently explained to me that The Netherlands was the last place she ever wanted to work because women in Dutch companies often were relegated to perfunctory roles. Historical precedents and cultural barriers helped to produce this environment. Dutch women never joined the workforce during the World Wars and current tax laws penalize families with more than one wage earner. Accordingly, there are fewer women per capita working in The Netherlands today than in Turkey, a largely Muslim nation that is run by a secular government that is increasingly encouraging women to participate in business.[3] Courageous leaders need to understand why some nations support women in the workplace and others actively discourage it in order to turn these disparities into opportunities, both in emerging markets and in the developed world.

Western countries can hardly be smug about their employment of women. There are only 12 women CEOs leading *Fortune* 500 companies. Women held only 14.8 percent of all available board seats of those 500 companies.[4] But this shortcoming is by no means limited to just the United States. Research conducted by Cass Business School on behalf of *Chief Executive Officer* magazine found that just 16 out of 1,450 companies around the world were headed by a female CEO.[5] In other words, there is much work still to be done. As depressing as those numbers seem, they are reality.

While I don't consider myself to be a radical feminist, I do think of myself as a radical *equalist*. Women are too often undervalued and underutilized, which adds up to countless lost economic opportunities. On this stop in our journey, our mission is to understand, by looking at both hard data and success stories, the critical role women can and will perform in the upcoming decades. Courageous leaders need to recognize the different ways the world's cultures embrace differences in gender.

Untapped Resources

To fail to pay attention to women's economic activities is both morally indefensible and economically absurd.

—Bradford Morse, U.N. Development Program[6]

Many of the emerging markets around the world have yet another untapped resource to spur their future growth: their women (see Figure 6.1). Progress is being made. There are some 1.2 billion women working in remunerative labor around the world—which is almost 200 million more than in 1997.[7] Yet, at a global level, less than 70 women are economically active compared to every 100 men.[8] Women make up less than 30 percent of the workforce in some countries and, in countries in which they do work, they are often consigned to agricultural jobs that require fewer skills and, therefore, pay lower wages.[9] As shown in Figure 6.1, from 2000 to 2002, women's overall share of managerial jobs ranged between only 20 and 40 percent, in 48 out of the 63 countries for which data were available.[10]

A trip that I took to Japan in the 1990s illustrated how that nation's decisionmakers' view of women led to labor shortages. I was part of a delegation of 12 leaders on a two-week mission to learn about the growing Japanese steel industry dynamics by visiting

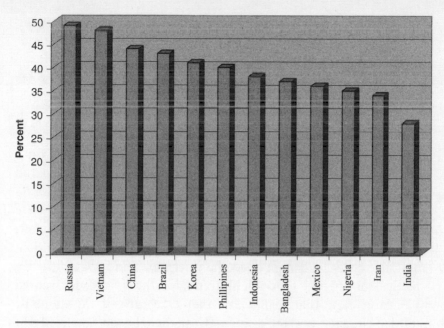

Figure 6.1 Percentage of Women in Workforce. *Data source:* World Bank Gender Stats, http://devdata.worldbank.org/ genderstats/home.asp.

business and government leaders and facilities in various cities and towns throughout the country. We visited Fukuoka City, which, with a population of more than one million people, had the ninth largest prefectural population in Japan. Fukuoka City, in fact, has had more exposure to new ideas from around the globe than most other cities in Japan. As the city leaders themselves note: "Because of its geographical proximity to the Chinese Continent and the Korean Peninsula, Fukuoka Prefecture and the whole of northern Kyushu has a long history of cultural exchange with the Asian Continent. It was the first region in Japan to come into contact with Asian cultures. A *Dazaifu* or local government office was established as early as 664 A.D. in Fukuoka in order to control Kyushu as a unit, as well as to take charge of the nation's foreign diplomatic and military affairs. It prospered as the political, economic, and cultural center of Kyushu."[11] In 1901, a government-run steel mill opened, starting the rise of the steel industry. As a result, Fukuoka became one of Japan's four major industrial centers.

During our cultural exchange, we visited the site of a former steel factory that now housed a Disneyland-type amusement park. Strangely, there were not many other visitors. When we met with the city's leaders, they lamented that so many of their young people flocked to Tokyo and other cities to find jobs, leaving a critical work shortage for the city. I asked these leaders if they ever considered addressing their workforce shortage by hiring women. A shuffling of papers ensued. Finally, the spokesman told me that I must have misunderstood. There was no workforce shortage in Fukuoka. Later, as we sipped wine together before leaving for another destination, an agitated city leader grabbed the interpreter and together they marched toward me. Through his translator, the civic leader wanted to make it clear that in his city, they take care of the mentally retarded, the aged, and the women. (Until then, I hadn't realized that women were among the infirm!) That was the message I received, loud and clear. If a city with the heritage and global opportunities that Fukuoka enjoys has leaders who think women need not apply for a job, imagine what it would be like in a city that is less prosperous or even more isolated.

Equal opportunity laws did not go into effect in Japan until 1986. To date the law's enactment is producing only minimal change. According to one analysis, "the purpose of the law was to harmonize women's home life and work life while improving women's welfare, defined as respect for motherhood, while not meaning sexual discrimination."[12] The law was aimed at opening more doors for women, not ensuring that they would receive an actual guarantee of employment. As researcher Karin Klenke concluded after reviewing Japanese equal opportunity laws: "It is not surprising that a large amount of women in the Japanese workforce feel discriminated against."[13] Economic pressure to utilize a valid labor pool is more likely to produce change than laws that reflect longstanding cultural biases. In Japan, women make up more than

51 percent of the total population, but only 41 percent of the work-force. But 20 years ago, Japanese women constituted only 36 percent of the workforce. Economic need is working to bring about change in ways that the law cannot.

The proportion of working women is even more disparate in India, where only 28 percent of the national labor force is made up of women. For comparison, 48 percent of the U.S. workforce is made up of women. As Klenke writes: "In India, women are constitution-ally equal to men, but are culturally defined as primarily responsible for the children and the home." Asian societies in general, Klenke found, continue to designate women with minority status.[14] Yet, countries like Singapore have embraced women in their workforce due to a recognition of women's value as workers under the leader-ship of Lee Kuan Yew who served as the first Prime Minister of the country from 1959 to 1990 and now serves as Minister Mentor to his son. The example of Singapore provides a reason for optimism.

Educating Women to Fuel Economic Growth

The difference between many Asian cultures and their rivals in the West is the society's commitment to educating their female pop-ulations. While residents of many western nations have come to take equal opportunities for women for granted, there are still far too many countries that preclude women from an opportunity for an education. Not only does this unnecessarily punish the female residents of those nations, it also impedes economic growth. Re-cent research compiled by Goldman Sachs found that if developing nations like Brazil, China, and India invested more in educating their female populations, they could achieve a "growth premium" in terms of the overall growth of their economies.[15] By increasing education levels, nations could see a 0.2 percent annual boost to their GDP growth, which could result in a 14 percent increase in per capita income by the year 2020. As the report's authors stated: "Educating girls and women leads to higher wages; a greater likelihood of working outside the home; lower fertility; reduced maternal and child mortality; and better health and education. The impact is felt not only in women's lifetimes, but also in the health, education and productivity of future generations."

Two types of education are required: primary and higher education. Increasing women's access to primary education to address the low literacy in many countries is an imperative first step to creating a better future. The midterm monitoring report for the Education For All by 2015 initiative shows progress is being made toward equal access to education for men and women.[16] Since the establishment of the Dakar Framework agreed to by many countries in 2000 to address the health and well-being of people living in emerging markets, primary school enrollment for girls increased by 36 percent in sub-Saharan Africa, 22 percent in South and West Asia, and 11 percent in Arab States. Plus the number of out-of-school children has declined from 96 million in 1999 to 72 million in 2005.

Educating women doesn't just make sense in terms of social change; it also makes for a good investment. In a study commissioned by the World Bank, researchers found that in the majority of developing countries, educating women resulted in greater economic returns than equivalent investments in males, particularly in higher levels of education, by more than 100 basis points: 9.8 percent returns for women compared to 8.7 percent returns for men (Figure 6.2).

The need for education and the acquisition of new skills for success in a global workforce are not limited to female workers in developing economies. A recent study of female professionals in 17 countries across Europe, Asia, North America, and South America found that just 43 percent of women professionals feel well equipped to compete in the modern economy.[17] Even more surprisingly, the survey found that businesswomen in emerging markets like South Africa, China, and Brazil were more confident than their developed-market counterparts in integrating with future economic trends—a

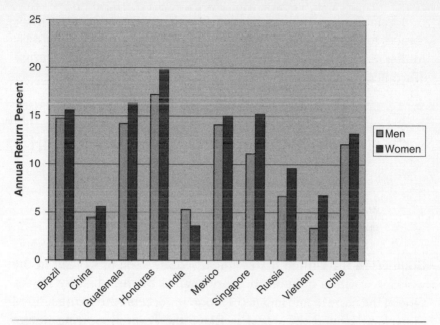

Figure 6.2   Returns to Education by Gender. *Data source:*
George Psacharopoulos and Harry Anthony Patrinos, "Returns to
Investment in Education: A Further Update," World Bank Policy
Research, working paper no. 2881, September 2002, Appendix A3.

potential warning sign that leaders of Western organizations are not
providing their female workers with the right kinds of skills and opportunities needed by the multi-polar world. The pace of this global
economy continues to accelerate. Leaders who are not developing
the skills of their employees and resources in their communities
are already slipping behind the competition. As Armelle Carminati-
Rabasse, the managing director of human capital and diversity at
Accenture told me: "Emerging-market economies are competing
with the collective dominance of the United States, Europe, and
Japan. In this increasingly competitive landscape, companies have a
mandate not only to adapt their business models, but also [to] equip
each of their employees with a wide array of skills—many of which
have not yet been demanded of executives."

Education and skills lead both to new opportunities and to new choices for women around the world. Let's take a look at some case studies of what happens when economic needs compel the inclusion of women in business.

Choices for Women Around the World

Brick walls are there for a reason. They let us prove how badly we want things.

—Randy Pausch[18]

Boomers in the United States addressed the issue of women in the workforce with a cultural memory shaped by their history books. One of the more iconic images of women workers both in the United States and around the world is Rosie the Riveter sporting denim overalls and exposed biceps who first appeared on the cover of the *Saturday Evening Post* on May 29, 1943.[19] Rosie became a symbol for the 18 million women who entered the U.S. workforce during World War II: double the number of women that were employed before the war in 1940. The women who stepped into unfamiliar roles overcame both sexism and racism to push the nation's industrial power forward to victory. However, once the war was over, public perception shifted and a woman was once again expected to stay at home where she could take care of her husband and children. Sally the Server, not Rosie the Riveter, became the ideal role model for women. No one ever made a poster of Sally, but American cultural icons like TV's Harriet Nelson, June Cleaver, and Laura Petrie made it clear that a woman's place was in the home.

But, beginning in the 1960s, when books like Betty Friedan's *The Feminine Mystique* were published, the perception of women in the workforce changed yet again.[20] By capturing the boredom and listlessness that so many women of the postwar generation felt, Friedan helped galvanize the notion that women, characterized by Lucy the Leader, could make choices about their careers just as their fathers, brothers, and husbands did. Today, 50 years later, women perform major roles in supporting their families financially. For instance, one survey taken in the United States found that nearly 66 percent of working women say they earn more than half their family's income, while about 55 percent of married women say they earn half or more of their family's income.[21] That means that women are just as capable of taking leadership roles in the interconnected economy as men.

Open the Doors to Opportunity

Women, as equal participants in the interconnected globe, have the choice to stand out by selecting when and how long they will work in organizations. As the authors of the 2008 "Employment Trends for Women" write: "While one should not assume that all women want to work, it is safe to say that women want to be given the same freedom as men to choose to work if they want to; and if they choose to work, they should have the same chance of finding decent jobs as men."[22] According to research from New York-based Center for Work-Life Policy, some 40 percent of women voluntarily step out of the workforce to take care of children or parents—not because of stress or unhappiness. And while 90 percent of those women who opt-out intend to return to work, only 75 percent actually do—and only some 40 percent actually go back to fulltime employment.[23] When less than one-half of the women who intended to rejoin the workforce fulltime did not do so, companies need new efforts to retain their trained and valued women employees to create a pipeline of women leaders in the twenty-first century. One effort is to find qualified women who left the workforce, but still have something to offer.

For example, in 2004 the board of directors of Sara Lee Corporation searched for a new chief executive officer. It employed an executive recruiter with the instruction to find the best candidate wherever she may be. In 2005, Brenda Barnes was named chairman and CEO of Sara Lee Corporation, a company with $12 billion in annual net sales covering 200 countries with 52,000 employees.

This move indicates a courageous willingness to confront increasingly archaic business proclivities. Brenda was hardly a typical CEO hire. In 1997, Brenda announced she was resigning her position as CEO of Pepsi-Cola North America to spend more time with her family. In making that decision, Brenda came under fire from other women, including news anchor Katie Couric, for "opting out" of the workforce.[24] One prominent headline read: "Goodbye, Superwoman." After a seven-year hiatus during which she served as a board member for several high-profile, successful companies and raised her family, Brenda had the last laugh when she joined Sara Lee Corporation. Brenda had the courage to stand out and do what she felt was best for her, and still return to the top job when she was ready. More women around the world are making their personal choices to *stand out* and become the role models for future generations to follow. But it takes enlightened policies and management to find, develop, and retain women leaders.

Role models matter. I first realized I could achieve my dream of being a chief financial officer (CFO) of an international company through my exposure to many men CFOs. I realized I had the same capabilities as well as the willingness to make personal sacrifices to pursue my objective as they had and I assumed that there must be some women who were also CFOs. Unfortunately, there were almost no women CFOs from whom I could learn. I was left to extrapolate from men's experiences to form a vague idea of how I might perform as a CFO. Even more important were the experiences of working with professional women in their leadership positions who provided role models for me.

Role models are important at all stages of a person's life. I'm reminded of the time that Arnold Weber, then the president of Northwestern University, wanted to get a handle on the attitudes and values of that university's female student body. The school conducted a deep survey of all the students and found that the majority of the freshmen women reported lower self-confidence scores than those of their male counterparts. Further research indicated low scores resulted from the lack of women role models and mentors who could help show the collegians how to overcome hurdles and develop their confidence through leadership skill development. President Weber's solution was to create what became the Council of 100, a group of 100 distinguished female alumnae who would serve as mentors during a woman's college years. The goal would be to give the college women the chance to ask questions and learn not only from success stories of the 100, but also from the mistakes they made. As one of the founding members, I not only had the chance to meet with some talented young women twice a year, I also worked with fellow alumnae, like Ruth Whitney. Whitney was editor-in-chief of *Glamour* magazine for 31 years where she was an innovator for controversial social and career issues. Before she passed away in 1999, the American Society of Magazine Editors' recognized her contributions with a Hall of Fame Award. She said, before she retired in 1998, "I always felt that I had a mission. I wanted to broaden the scope of a magazine to go with women's lives."[25] For example, for the cover of *Glamour* in 1972, Whitney insisted on having Beverly Johnson, the first African American model on any of the seven major women's magazines. By reading *Glamour*, Whitney hoped her readers would not only learn about social and economic concerns, but also become better citizens of the world. She was a role model for me as well as the collegians. Her impact on the publishing industry reached many corners of the world and changed social trends. Business leaders can produce social change, often times more effectively than politicians.

Building Global Capabilities

As Karen Hughes, the Under Secretary for Public Diplomacy and Public Affairs, noted in a speech in Honolulu, Hawaii: "Women are increasingly agents of change, arbiters of peace and reconciliation, and advocates of education and health."[26] In that speech, she noted some of the female luminaries around the world, like Michelle Bachelet, a former political prisoner who is now the president of Chile, Angela Merkel, a former physicist and the first woman chancellor of Germany, and Ellen Sirleaf Johnson, the president of

Liberia (the country once known as among the worst places in the world to be a woman) who are creating new opportunities through political change.

But women are steadily changing the cultural dynamics of the workplace as well. Recent entrants into the ranks of female chief executives include Indra Nooyi at Pepsi, Monika Ribar at the Swiss logistics group Panalpina, and Mia Brunnell at the Swedish investment bank Kinnevik.[27] When these women assume leadership positions, they tend to make changes that influence the way their organizations embrace work-life balance among other business priorities, says Avivah Wittenberg-Cox, the Paris-based managing partner of consultancy Diafora and founder of the European Professional Women's Network.[28] Creating work-life balance options is a step toward keeping women in the workforce because, in many cultures, the woman is still the person primarily responsible for family care.

In this new era of globalization, it is likely that female employees are already interacting with people outside their own cultures and borders. Each of these interactions changes, incrementally, the perception of what women can do. Deb Morrin, as chief financial officer for a company that was a world leader in dental instruments based in Chicago, worked with that company's managing director for Europe, U.A.E., and Africa who was based in Germany. At first, he did not want anything to do with her, evincing hostility to a woman in that role. He screamed at her, "You don't even have the basic understanding of how we do business and can't possibly help." He complained that the division was required to buy all of its manufactured goods from the United States at a time when the dollar was strong, making the cost of goods of the products in the local European and African markets much higher than any of the competitors. Morrin met with him in Germany and calmly developed an income statement showing results in constant dollars and shared this with the top U.S. management so that it would understand the German-based businesses. She also worked with the managing director to develop a budget based in Euros and created a bonus plan based on non-U.S. standards that was acceptable to the corporate office. As a result, the managing director invited Morrin to work with him to negotiate an acquisition of a division of Planmeca, based in Finland. They both made the acquisition presentation to the owners and executive management team in Chicago. Afterward, he told her how much he enjoyed working with her and continued to rely on her judgment.[29]

A recent survey of 4,100 business professionals across 17 countries indicated that, "While only 39 percent of the respondents worldwide work for organizations with international operations, 69 percent of respondents have working relationships outside of their country."[30] Imagine how many contacts with men in developing countries are made every day by these female professionals. Companies that recognize and embrace diverse leadership styles by offering opportunities for advancement and management will improve their own organizations as well as their financial results. Women need to exert their power to contribute to the business objectives and make a difference in order for employers to want to retain them. After all, if you generate revenue or cost savings for an organization to justify your salary, you are a desirable resource.

Women leaders often see the use of power more as a masculine trait. Women must be comfortable with power and use it productively. Nancy J. Adler, a professor of international management at McGill University in Montreal, encourages women to use power to exact positive change.[31] Using power demands the courage to:

- See reality as it actually is—to "collude against illusion" even when society and colleagues reject your perceptions.
- Imagine a better world—to imagine the possibility even when society and colleagues consider such possibilities naïve, unattainable, or foolish.
- Communicate reality and possibility so powerfully that others can't help but move forward toward a better future.

One of the best ways to achieve future goals is to measure results over time and focus on how inclusion will improve the availability of talent.

What Is Measured Happens

*The equality of women in the workforce is no longer a political luxury.
It has become a competitive necessity.*

—Rosabeth Moss Kanter[32]

Shining attention on and responding to the current situation helps us understand that while some nations have traditionally ignored or failed to value diversity in the workplace, the needs of the global economy are producing change. Ironically, in today's world, working outside the United States may actually provide better opportunities for women. In a market society, measuring and quantifying data creates the dimensions of a problem and an opportunity. One way we will be able to track the progress we're making toward including more women in the global workforce is to start looking at the numbers.

As we start to look at results, we see that when women are given the same opportunities and access to things like capital, they produce. Let's first consider emerging market activity that reflects the rising impact of micro-finance projects or so-called "micro-loans" where small amounts of money are made available to potential entrepreneurs in developing countries. These programs have been a boon to women around the world because more than 60 percent of the world's 70 million micro-borrowers are women.[33] For example, of the 28,000 loans made in Afghanistan, 75 percent have gone to women. When the results of these loans are tracked, we see that not only do they result in a boost to economic growth; they also improve the social status of the women within their society. Studies show that women who take advantage of these loans become more involved in their families' decision making, more independent and geographically mobile, more politically and legally aware, and more knowledgeable about both their own health and that of their family members.[34] Another example is Chile, where it is estimated that there are about 513,000 women entrepreneurs, equal to 33 percent of all entrepreneurs in the nation. Three years ago the percentage was just 20 percent. If that growth rate continues through 2010, there will be just as many female entrepreneurs as males and women will account for more than 50 percent of all new jobs created in the country. The rise of women in the workplace can be attributed to "the profound progress in equal access by women to the Chilean educational system in the last 20 years, which has helped better incorporate the capabilities of women to the country's development," says Olga Pizarro, professor and researcher for the Center for Entrepreneurship of Universidad del Desarrollo and co-author of the report that studied the role of women entrepreneurs in the country.[35] In other words, cultures that make smart investments in their women through education and entrepreneurship reap significant returns throughout their society.

HSBC management has taken a lead in investing in women in Asia. While in Paris and again in Mumbai, I had the pleasure of speaking with Naina Kidwai, the group general manager and country head of India for HSBC. On both occasions, she impressed me as someone who knew how to deliver results, supported the training programs in which I was involved, and motivated men and women to embrace the values of HSBC. Later, I discovered she has made a significant impact at promoting women while being the first woman to head a foreign bank in India. According to Kidwai, "When I was deputy CEO, I was appointed to head the diversity initiative. We set up task forces across the country—with groups of 10 or 15 people, and with both men and women—who met over three months and came up with ideas on how to make the workplace more diverse. We have a very young workforce, and at any given point, we had some young mothers who would not come to work because they were breastfeeding their babies. No one had thought of it before, but they needed an additional facility at work. It was just a token—these restrooms aren't even used a whole lot—but it was a good 'hygiene factor.' These are among the reasons why HSBC is one of the most preferred employers in India today, apart from the fact that we provide global careers. We're giving women plenty of space and time."[36]

HSBC works with Duke Corporate Education to create week-long middle manager and executive programs to develop leaders, men and women, throughout their world network. The need to make these investments is spurred by the need to compete in a global economy. As major corporations develop their business in emerging markets, they encourage indigenous cultures to reconsider old prejudices and tradition in order to benefit economically.

To use the hidden talent of women and keep them in the workforce, organizations need to actively create more role models and initiatives to encourage women to develop and leverage the opportunities offered by the interconnected globe. Events by companies and nations held on the International Women's Day, March 8, continue to garner attention and momentum throughout the world. In recent years, I have participated in events from Bangalore to London on this day, seeing and feeling the mobilization of public opinion and international action toward the advancement of gender equality as a fundamental human right.

Impact of Women Board Members and Executives

Although regulating change in a heterogeneous world is difficult given the multiple and disparate priorities of citizens, there is an example of one country in which legislators passed regulation to make a marked difference in women representation at the highest levels of business. In 2003, Norway passed a law that required companies to fill 40 percent of their corporate board seats with women by 2008. The impetus for the law was that in 1993, women only held 6 percent of the nation's corporate board positions. "If organic growth is 3 percent every 10 years, it would have taken us 100 years to get to 40 percent," said Elin Hurvenes, the founder of the Professional Board Forum, an organization that connects prospective female board members with board members involved in board selection.[37] While Norway's law had its desired impact, it has also achieved an unintended consequence; it has spurred copycats throughout Europe. Countries like Denmark, Estonia, Greece, and Sweden have implemented quotas and similar legislation. The key point is not the legislation itself, but the fact that as soon as measurements are taken seriously, things begin to change. This is a universally successful approach for a global leader who wants to be relevant in the interconnected world.

One token woman is not sufficient to make a difference, but evidence shows that those companies with several women board members report better financial results. Research conducted by Catalyst, a nonprofit corporate membership research and advisory organization, has found, in fact, companies with more women board members outperform those with fewer female representatives (see Figure 6.3). I have a saying regarding women board members: "One is good, two is better, and three or more is best to keep the company out of harm's way and to promote change." With one woman, she may wonder if her informed opinion is on track or relevant to the majority of members in the boardroom. With two women, they may talk among themselves and act carefully and more slowly than the majority. With three women, in a group of 8 to 10 board members, women have a shared voice in the room and command significant weight in the decision-making process. The point is not to exclude men. The point is to create an atmosphere in which different points of view can be expressed, heard, and considered to create a thoughtful and informed decision for strategic action.

The pace of change in terms of global organizations adding female executives has been slow as well. Just as in the United States, women hold only 2 percent of the chief executive positions at the 100 largest companies in the European Union—while there is but a single female CFO among those same 100 firms.[38]

Nurturing Future Global Leaders

Part of the responsibility of current leaders is to groom the next generation of global talent. As Sarah Hunt, a managing director of the London-based recruiting company EquityFD has said: "Women who have made it to the top of the ladder have an important role

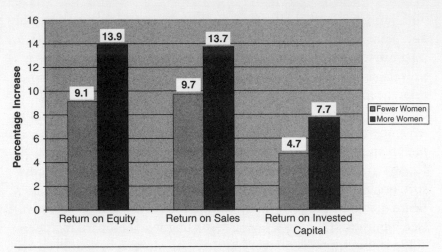

Figure 6.3   Impact of Women Board Members.   *Data source:* Sheli Z. Rosenberg, "Why Aren't There More Women on Boards?" *Directorship*, April–May 2008, p. 56.

to play, offering advice to those still climbing." In addition to advice, women and enlightened men have a role: *hiring and developing women* who have integrity and potential. One of the key aspects of grooming global women leaders is to give them the experience of working outside their home country or "cultural comfort zone." Women, just like men, greatly benefit from the experience of learning about and integrating with disparate cultures. Be alert to avoid scenarios like this one penned by *Fortune* columnist Ann Fisher:

> *You, a hotshot of either sex, show up alone in Tokyo to meet with the head honchos of a prospective joint-venture partner. You don't know how to say "hello" or "thank you" in Japanese, you don't have a proper business card, and you plop yourself down in any old seat at the conference table. Pretty soon your counterparts won't look you in the eye, and before you know it, you're on the plane home and the deal is off. How did you blow it? Probably by not knowing enough—or caring enough—to learn the basics of the culture you were flying into. Sayonara, baby.[39]*

In an essay that appears in the book, *Enlightened Power*, Nancy J. Adler writes of the important role that working abroad has on women's career trajectories. From her research, she found that while some 40 percent of managers in North America were women, women made up only 3 percent of the workforce being sent abroad on expatriate assignments. "No matter how much emphasis North Americans placed on employment equity, especially for the increasing number of women managers, it seemed highly unlikely that anyone would be promoted into senior leadership of the next generation of global companies if he or she had not the opportunity to work abroad."[40]

Women must convince the decision makers to ignore the three myths of sending women abroad:

Myth 1: Women do not want to become international managers.

Myth 2: Companies refuse to send women abroad.

Myth 3: Foreigners' prejudice against women renders women ineffective.

Not only are these three myths false, Adler's research found that of the women managers who did go abroad, 97 percent of those women succeeded in their assignments, regardless of the country. In fact, 42 percent of those surveyed said that being a woman was actually an *advantage* in their service abroad. Since women leaders are more often interested in making a positive impact with their careers as opposed to making purely financial gains, working abroad actually gives them new opportunities to see the impact of their decisions in a new light. As the late Anita Roddick, founder of the Body Shop, once wrote: "Leaders in the business world should aspire to be true planetary citizens. They have global responsibilities since their decisions affect not just the world of business, but world problems of poverty, national security and the environment."[41] The lesson learned, then, is that companies that overlook the potential of sending their female workers abroad do so at their own peril.

Key Points to Consider

- What is the progress your organization is making at developing, retaining, and promoting women into global leadership roles, within its borders and with those other organizations or people with whom you partner?

- Are there opportunities for your organization to leverage women in a leadership capacity? What can your organization do to give its female members more tools to compete in the interconnected economy?

- Does your organization create developmental opportunities for women within the critical divisions, client assignments or indispensable functions? Have you identified experiences so women can serve in the C-suite?

- Can you identify women in your organization that you think have high CQ scores? If so, what can you do to develop and support them to compete in the global world?

- Is there potential for you to measure the impact of women within your organization? If not, is there a way to create such a metric?

The Next Stop

Women may look different from men, but they have the same global leadership capabilities. Now that we have a better sense of how some business leaders in our interconnected globe have ignored this critical talent resource—and demonstrated the ways they and national policies can reverse that mistake—we can now continue our journey. Our next stop is to examine the different shareholders that drive decisions in organizations around the world—far from and near to their local economies.

CHAPTER

7

Shareholder Interests

Today's global leaders need to understand the motivations of global investors. For much of the twentieth century, foreign direct investments (FDI) channeled capital in and out of U.S.-based companies. U.S. companies accounted for 85 percent of the new FDI between 1945 and the mid-1960s.[1] Representatives from developed markets primarily invested in other developed markets or established local facilities to use the cheap labor available in allied developing nations. U.S. manufacturers would build plants in Mexico while Japanese carmakers made investments in Southeast Asia.[2] Today, however, these capital flows have become multidirectional, as capital from companies and governments based in emerging markets make investments outside of their home country.

The bid of $23 billion from the Indian company, Mittal Steel, for Luxembourg-based rival Arcelor in January 2006 reveals this new dynamic. Prior to the acquisition launch, the Mittal family controlled 85 percent of Mittal Steel through its voting rights. When the deal, after an acrimonious six-month battle, was consummated at $33.7 billion, Arcelor shareholders owned 50.5 percent and the Mittal family 43 percent of the combined company. This merger created a steel producer that makes more than 100 million tons of steel a year—roughly 10 percent of the world's total output. Several years ago, no one would have imagined that capital from an Indian family and a French-listed public company would combine to create the largest steel company in the world, which is now called ArcelorMittal. New capital resources determine new patterns of investment. Much of ArcelorMittal investments in the past two years have been in plants in India and other emerging markets.

More money is being invested in foreign markets than ever before. The multidirectional nature of its flow has resulted in a burgeoning global capital market in which investors have many options from which to choose. The Morgan Stanley International emerging market index passed $2 trillion for the first time in 2006 and international investors plowed $61.4 billion into emerging market equities. In 2007, developing countries as a whole received a net inflow of $196.9 billion, with official net outflows of $128.5 billion.[3] As Figure 7.1 shows, emerging markets, as a whole, no longer experience net capital exports, but now are net importers of capital. Boards of directors, as representatives of shareholders, decide on major

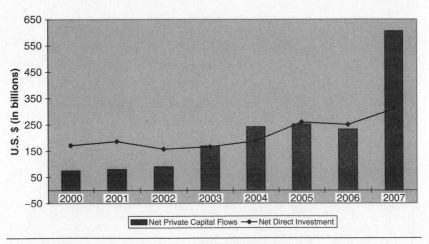

Figure 7.1   Capital Trends in Emerging Markets. *Data source:* International Monetary Fund, "World Economic Outlook Database," April 2008, www.imf.org.

capital flows such as acquisitions, seeking to invest capital in companies and countries with high probable returns on the investment. As the authors of the report titled "The Rise of the Emerging-Market Multinational," wrote: "As liberalization and technological advances drive deeper integration of global capital markets, emerging-market investors are increasingly prominent, boasting a growing share of both foreign direct investment and portfolio capital flows."[4]

This trend has also had the effect of changing the tenor of the global merger and acquisition market. As capital begins to find its way into the coffers of companies based in emerging markets, those companies in turn have begun using their new resources to expand. In 1995, just 20 of the companies on the Fortune Global 500 were based in emerging markets. Today, more than 70 of the world's biggest companies are based in countries like China, India, and Brazil.[5] The 100 largest emerging market multinational companies (EMMs), held $471 billion in foreign assets in 2005, a 40 percent increase from 2004. Companies based in emerging markets are turning their eyes toward acquisitions in both the developed and developing worlds to fuel their growth (Figure 7.2). In 2006 alone, deals initiated by EMMs totaled more than $1.2 trillion. EMMs undertook over 1,000 significant merger and acquisition (M&A) transactions in 2006, a sharp rise from previous years.

This flurry of activity has resulted in the emergence of new global business giants, not from the developed world, but from emerging markets. An example is PetroChina, a government-funded company that debuted on the Hong Kong stock exchange in 2007, garnering a market capitalization of more than $1 trillion—the largest public company in the world at the time.[6] Another formidable world player in capital markets is the Tata Group, the multinational conglomerate based in Mumbai, India, which, with revenues of U.S. $55 billion, is the largest private company in India.[7] The Tata Group operates in more than 85 countries across six continents and its 98 companies export products and services in seven business sectors to 80 nations. Twenty-seven of its companies are publicly listed with a market capitalization of U.S. $64.4 billion at the end of May 2008. Companies that form a major part of the group include Tata Steel,

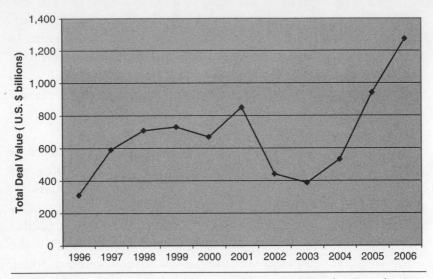

Figure 7.2   Cross-Border Merger and Acquisition by Developing Nations. *Data source:* United Nations Conference on Trade and Development, www.unctad.org.

Corus Steel, Tata Consultancy Services, Tata Tea, Tata Power, Tata Communications, Taj Hotels, and Tata Motors, which most recently purchased the Jaguar and Land Rover brands from Ford Motor Co. In other words, the global face of business is changing and it is the shareholders of these new sources of capital that are beginning to shake the globe.

What's the Fuss about Globalization?

Professor Peter Drucker predicted many of the major developments of the past 40 years. I was fortunate to be part of a small group of 20 executives when he gave one of his last lectures at the age of 92. He began our discussion by asking, "What's the fuss about globalization?"[8] His overall theme was that competition can come from anywhere in an interconnected market. Drucker identified the five distinct economic cycles in recent history. Many casual observers recognize the first three of these five recent cycles: the Industrial Age in the United Kingdom in the early nineteenth century, the emergence of the economic engines in the late nineteenth century in the United States and Germany, and the "Asian Miracle" of the mid-twentieth century. The last two are less familiar and have occurred in rapid succession: the rise of Eastern European and Pacific Rim economies in the latter part of the twentieth century followed by the twenty-first-century development of transnational companies in countries like Mexico, Brazil, and India. As has been noted earlier, not everyone adjusts well to change. Anyone seeing his economic power threatened by the interconnected economy will try to resist and refuse to participate even in the inevitable, at least initially. Those that feel the most stings raise the loudest objections to the changes taking place. Let's consider two such groups: labor unions and French farmers.

Unions can't accept the steady decline of wealth generation from the manufacturing goods industry. U.S. labor unions capture the lion's share of their economic power through their control of pension assets and union fees, both highly dependent on membership figures. In 2006, union membership fell to 15.4 million workers or 12 percent of total employees, continuing its decline. The percentages of employees in unions are down from 20 percent in 1983 and from 35 percent in the 1950s.[9] In manufacturing, the core of organized labor, union membership dropped to a new low of 11.7 percent in 2006. Instead of imposing protectionist laws to protect these jobs, one possible solution would be for labor leaders to reform education so Americans can become reskilled and participate in the new economy of technology and services.

Ironically, as the number of farmers in a country like France declines, their political voice has increased. Only 3.5 percent of the French are farmers, but the rest of the French do not protest the agricultural subsidies and tariffs that make their food more expensive and undercut the livelihoods of farmers in the emerging economies. The main reason for the French acceptance of the minority voice is that the European Union's Common Agricultural Policy (CAP) has been very profitable for France as a whole. The CAP spending of

$85 billion in 2007 represents 40 percent of the overall EU budget, with France receiving the greatest share (20 percent) of the subsidies even though other countries like Germany, Great Britain, and The Netherlands are greater net contributors to the overall budget.[10] Much of this money is concentrated in the hands of the main agricultural unions who are so determined to hold onto their powers that they will use violence when necessary. The political influence of farmers extends to the French Senate; "As senators elected by local officials from France's 36,000 communes, the countryside is overrepresented."[11] In spite of the public sentiment of saving the rural ambience and holding onto the historic roots of the farming community, the biggest French farms swallow up the vast majority of the European Union (EU) agricultural subsidies.[12] As technology produces greater productivity, less people are needed in both manufacturing and agriculture. With this new age of multinationals and technology, the world operates more and more as one economy. Assuming you can export your production, there is no such thing as a local market. The farming subsidies of developed nations exacerbate the volatility in and put pressure on agricultural economies in the emerging markets just as the trade barriers regarding manufacturing goods create distortions. In an interconnected world, even in the face of entrenched interests, a global leader must recognize the unintended consequences of politically motivated economic decisions rather than free market decisions.

When EMMs go on acquisition sprees, such as China's Lenovo purchasing IBM's PC business or India's Tata Group acquiring Jaguar and Land Rover from Ford Motor Co., eyebrows rise up in surprise. Voices of nationalistic pride and champions of the status quo tend to see such maneuvers as destructive. However, these acquisitions frequently represent the flow of capital and jobs often into the very country where workers are resisting the change. But there is a change of what type of investments foreigners are making in the United States. Reviewing the past 30 years of FDI data provided by the U.S. government (excluding treasury securities), foreign investment in U.S.-based assets through 2001 were mainly in stocks and less in corporate debt. Then, in 2002, a shift occurred. As Table 7.1 illustrates, foreign investment now seeks more

Table 7.1 Foreign Assets in U.S. Securities

Asset	Percentages of Total Foreign Assets								
	1998	1999	2000	2001	2002	2003	2004	2005	2006
Bonds	38	35	41	48	55	50	51	52	51
Corporate stocks	62	65	59	52	45	50	49	48	49

Note: Proportion computed by asset class, excluding U.S. Treasury securities.
Source: Bureau of Economic Analysis.

security through investments in corporate debt rather than risking their capital in equity.

These figures suggest the need for leaders to both have a strategy to *attract* investors, to *design* the organization, and to *align* its processes and practices with the changes in global investing.

At the other end of the spectrum of acquisitions, many companies choose to separate roles from the traditional headquarters, keeping the core business functions, often outsourcing others. The new realities of the global economy show that companies are increasingly disaggregating themselves, breaking up into different business or functional units to take advantage of new sources of talent or cost efficiencies. That means that acquisitions have become a two-way street, on which companies from both developed and emerging markets look to each other for help. Microsoft has been making investments and acquisitions in China for more than 10 years. Nokia, a Finnish company, has its R&D team based in the United Kingdom and its assembly plants in China. Different geographic areas each have their own appeal. Michael Reid, author of *Forgotten Continent*, writes: "If China is becoming the world's workshop and India its back office, Brazil is its farm—and potentially its center of environmental services."[13] Centers of excellence are created by specialization. These hubs of knowledge have employees interacting, which quickens the pace of adopting best practices and advances innovation. Just as this occurs within a company, for example, one area focuses on textile manufacturing and another focuses on high-technology ventures, geographic areas too are starting to specialize.

Leaders can assuage the fears of their employees, especially if they are shareholders, and fellow citizens by highlighting success stories created by healthy foreign investments. As chief financial officer for Hannaford Bros. Co. in the late 1990s, I had a bird's eye view of one such investment and divestment. In the 1980s, Sobeys, Inc., a 150-year-old Canadian grocery chain based in Nova Scotia, acquired 25.2 percent of the U.S. supermarket chain Hannaford Bros. Co., based in Scarborough, Maine. Hannaford management benefited from the counsel and stability of Sobeys' board members. The teams exchanged many ideas across borders that helped both companies keep innovative and highly competitive in their local markets.

Then, in 1998, Sobeys purchased Oshawa Group, which tripled the size of the company and created the second largest food distributor in Canada. As a direct result of this purchase, Sobeys also acquired a great deal of debt and the company needed to monetize its investment in Hannaford Bros. In other words, anyone who was following Hannaford's major investor would have realized that the world significantly changed for the investor and subsequently, the investee. We auctioned Hannaford Bros. Co, a Fortune 500 company, to the highest bidder in 1999. When the Belgian company Delhaize met the price, Hannaford ceased to be an independent company. Some members of Hannaford's management became leaders of the combined larger company, others left for better opportunities. Sobeys received cash to pay down their debts and the capital to add additional stores to grow its international business footprint. Long-term shareholders, including many of the rank and file employees, also saw the value of their shares grow from $16 to $71 over a five-year period: a true win-win transaction.

Overcoming New Tensions

The voices of negativity get louder and more defensive when the stakes appear higher, particularly if an EMM's country of origin isn't as well known or trusted as Canada. In other words, it becomes a question of *who* is really controlling the purse strings and *what* their motivations might be. In today's world, "security" has become a prime buzzword not only for politicians, but also for investors. For example, when DP World, a subsidiary of Dubai World, a holding company owned by the government of Dubai in the United Arab Emirates (UAE), acquired the U.K.-based Peninsular and Oriental Steam Navigation Company (P&O) in 2006, the company inherited the management of several key U.S. port facilities, including those in New York, New Jersey, Philadelphia, Baltimore, New Orleans, and Miami. Yet, despite the friendly ties between the governments of the United States and the UAE, both public and political outcry over a Middle East-based company operating U.S. port facilities caused DP World to sell off P&O's American operations to American International Group's asset management division, Global Investment Group, for an undisclosed sum.[14]

Ed Merkle, who heads up security at the Virginia Port Authority (VPA), once told me that the bigger enemy is thievery at the wharf—not where the headquarters of the operating company might be. Based in Norfolk, Virginia, the VPA operates four general cargo facilities and uses security measures to keep losses at a minimum. With lower costs and less crime than ports in Long Beach, California, the VPA attracts many shippers and manufacturers, even though the time at sea for China cargo increases by eight days. Maersk, the largest shipper in the world representing 26 percent of the Danish GDP, for instance, chose to lease space at the VPA terminals. By embracing low-cost methods and attracting customers from around the world, the VPA and correlating maritime industry create 463,000 jobs and revenues of $41 billion for Virginia. As with any other business transaction, customers will make their choices based on some combination of cost and service. DP Ports also runs a world-class operation. Yet, when it came to make a choice about a company like DP Ports, more than a few leaders chose to make a nationalist political point rather than an economic one. This hurts the U.S.'s competitive position in the global world because inefficient costs impose adverse conditions on users of American ports.

The change in the flows of capital now emanating from these emerging markets creates new tensions for today's global leaders. When organizations begin to make investments in emerging markets, parceling out manufacturing and R&D activities, for instance, there is the potential for tension like that caused by DP World's acquisition of P&O. But that failed deal was more than just a one-time phenomenon. Middle Eastern investors in particular have been moving aggressively to diversify their holdings by making investments overseas. One area of interest is U.S. media companies where, for example, movie studio Warner Bros. Entertainment struck up a multibillion-dollar strategic partnership with the Abu Dhabi Media Co. while Sony, News Corp., Time Warner, and Disney have all benefited from similar investments from the Middle East.[15]

Part of the job of today's global leaders, therefore, is to identify the key shareholders who will shape a company's destiny and then manage the potential implications of those decisions. The funds will continue to grow and help keep liquidity in the financial markets. Without this capital, many companies as varied as steel producers to media content creators would fail. To get a better idea of the most influential among these shareholders, we need to understand the role of governments and their investment vehicles.

Role of State Capitalism

One of the common themes of doing business around the world is socialized or state capital. In short, this theme describes the critical role that some government policies and direct investments play in the global economy. While this is indeed a form of capitalism, it is far from a free market. Airbus, for instance, receives political and, controversially, financial support from governments such as France, Germany, and the United Kingdom—which, to some, creates an uneven playing field. Another example of a government-supported business is CITGO, the Venezuelan petroleum giant. I often wonder how many Americans actively consider and decide where to buy gas—particularly from a station owned by a declared enemy of the

United States. Leaders of global organizations must be aware of "state capitalism" and how it alters relationships. Given the recent uncertainty, volatility, and weakness of the Western capital markets, there is a strong likelihood of an acceleration of new flows of capital. Excessive scrutiny of the source of government capital erects a hurdle and will put developed market organizations at a disadvantage. Investors will choose to move their capital to markets where it is easier to do business.

There is a distinct difference in how U.S.-based investors value government-backed companies as opposed to their European colleagues. My experience serving as a chief financial officer of both U.S.-based companies like Hannaford as well as the French-based Bic Group, served as a basis for an article published in 2001 in which I described the differences in the investors of these two companies.[16] Only seven years ago, I could write about an American company, owned largely by Americans, and a European company, owned largely by Europeans, and come to conclusions accordingly. U.S. investors tend to be attracted to undervalued and perhaps misunderstood companies that produce consistent, reliable results. In other words, American investors love bargains. I call this the "consumer consumption model of investing." Conversely, European investors look for companies that generate cash and have a good reputation in their country of origin. The real difference, though, is that European investors are particularly attracted to companies that have government backing—something I call "socialized capital." Even if a company is highly leveraged or is under fire for a scandal, European investors like to know that the government will be there to bail it out.

Emerging Market Multinationals Go Global

Since many EMMs are, in fact, backed by the government in their country of origin, investors need to learn about the role that an emerging market government may be taking in a company before leaping into an investment as a shareholder. In China, just about every enterprise operates with at least the tacit support of the government, while many companies receive direct financial and political aid. One example is an upstart Chinese automaker called Great Wall Motor Company, Ltd., based in Hebei Province, south of Beijing. While Great Wall produced only 108,000 vehicles in 2007—about half of what Toyota churns out in a week—the company is growing rapidly. Generating revenue of more than $1 billion with healthy profit margins, it is the first privately owned Chinese automaker to list on the Hong Kong stock exchange. It has the capacity to produce 400,000 vehicles a year and the auto components used in its vehicles. In the first quarter of 2008, the company publicly announced its intentions to begin exporting cars to Western nations like the United States. The source of funding the company's expansion plans is unclear. Though the company raised more than $200 million in a public listing on the Hong Kong exchange in 2003, it has become more dependent on bank borrowings. On the other hand, observers note that, "the sympathetic eye of the central government and recent visits from high-ranking politburo members may have smoothed the way."[17] Depending on an investor's perspective, the fact that the Chinese government is taking a direct role in creating a major automobile company with an appetite for exporting could be an attractive option. It could also be a wake-up call for other automobile competitors and a concern for their financial future.

Another example of a government-backed enterprise is the Commercial Aircraft Corporation of China (CACC), launched in May 2008. Its mission, as stated by Wen Jiabao, China's prime minister, is nothing less than to mount a challenge to the global duopoly of Europe's Airbus and America's Boeing.[18] The Chinese government clearly intends to develop a strong high-end manufacturing base for large aircraft—and is willing to commit billions of dollars to the effort. Leaders in the aviation industry need to be prepared for this new company's entry in the marketplace. The role of government money is not limited to steering the fortunes of those companies residing within political borders. A recent concern for the U.S. Congress, for example, is a flurry of recent large investments made in the U.S. financial service sector by foreign governments through financial vehicles called *sovereign wealth funds*—a new source of influence that emerging market economies are using to gain influence in the interconnected economy.

Rise of Sovereign Wealth Funds

An important and often controversial subset of state-sponsored capitalism that has risen in prominence of late is sovereign wealth funds (SWFs). These are government-owned vehicles that make investments in private-sector corporations. The first SWF created on record is credited to the Pacific island nation of Kiribati in 1956, which used it as a tool to manage the income it received from its phosphate deposits.[19] But it is the investments made by SWFs in American equities over the past year in particular which have drawn increased interest and scrutiny as to both the opportunities and the threats associated with these increasingly prominent sources of capital. It is now estimated that all SWFs combined represent about $2.5 trillion; by 2015, though, observers like Brian G. Cartwright, the general counsel of the Securities and Exchange Commission, predict that that number could rise to $12 trillion in investable assets.[20] The SWF money has been increasingly put to work, as some 127 transactions worth more than $139 billion took place between 2006 and 2007—with 37 of those transactions worth at least $1 billion.[21] According to Peter Morici, an economist and professor at the University of Maryland School of Business, governments in China and the Middle East already have enough capital on hand to purchase as much as 20 percent of the U.S. equities market.[22] As is evident in Table 7.2, SWFs come from all over the world—including the United States—and can bring an enormous amount of capital to bear. As the authors of Accenture's report on EMMs wrote: "As EMMs continue to expand, a new phenomenon has arisen. Sovereign wealth funds—state-owned investment organizations that invest in other countries—are contributing to the broadening and diversification of the global investor base. These burgeoning funds, whose values have been boosted by surging commodity prices and current

Table 7.2   The 10 Largest Sovereign Wealth Funds

Country	Fund Name	Launch Year	Value (in U.S. $ billions)
UAE (Abu Dhabi)	ADIA	1976	625
Norway	Government Pension Fund—Global	1990	322
Singapore	GIC	1981	215
Kuwait	Kuwait Investment Authority	1953	213
China	China Investment Corporation	2007	200
Russia	Stabilization Fund	2004	127.5
Singapore	Temasek	1974	108
Qatar	Qatar Investment Authority	2005	60
Algeria	Revenue Regulation Fund	2000	44.4
U.S. (Alaska)	Permanent Reserve Fund	1976	40.2

Source: Aaron Bernstein, "How Cross-Border Government Investments Are Shaking Up Western Economies," *Directorship*, April–May 2008, p. 35.

account surpluses, are starting to shape the flows of capital from emerging markets to developed markets."[23]

The trouble is that there seems to be more reactionary fear than understanding of SWFs. In fact, few people outside of the financial services industry gave much thought to the concept of SWFs until they took active roles in the bailout of struggling Western financial institutions. The bailouts produced a lot of uproar and headlines about SWFs, not unlike that raised in the 1980s when Japanese investors took positions in trophy assets like Rockefeller Center, Columbia Pictures, and Pebble Beach, the famed California golf course, but little substantive reasons to reject the capital needed to keep the enterprises viable. It seems citizens, when aware of news, get skittish over the notion of foreigners buying what they consider national assets. For instance, a study undertaken by Public Strategies, a research and consulting firm, found that 55 percent of all Americans think that investments made by foreign governments harm the national security of the United States.[24] At the same time, Ben Bernanke, the chairman of the Federal Reserve Bank, has openly encouraged financial institutions to "remain proactive in their capital raising efforts—doing so will help the broader economy."[25] The facts support Bernanke because foreign investors spent some $414 billion acquiring stakes in both public and private U.S. companies in 2007 according to research conducted by Thomson Financial, a 90-percent increase from 2005.[26]

SWFs are emerging as an essential source of capital in the global economy, but leaders still need to put pressure on some to make the ultimate goals and intentions of those funds clearer. The key for global leaders is to understand both the positive and potentially negative aspects of courting capital from SWFs.

On the positive side of the equation, SWFs represent the ultimate fluidity of capital movement. With the aid of capital like this, organizations can fund their growth across borders and successfully tap the new opportunities emerging in the interconnected economy. As Warren Buffett, head of Berkshire Hathaway and known as the "Oracle of Omaha" noted: "Our trade equation guarantees massive foreign investment in the United States. When we force-feed $2 billion daily to the rest of the world, they [sic] must invest in something here. Why should we complain when they choose stocks over bonds?"[27]

On the flip side, many SWFs are cloaked in some degree of mystery. A clear goal in making their role better accepted and clearer to other shareholders is to make the inner workings of their operations more transparent to the outside world. The U.S. Congress found the need to openly question a flurry of investments made by SWFs in the U.S. financial sector. It passed legislation called the National Security Foreign Investment Reform and Strengthened Transparency Act. Lawmakers created this act and a series of what were positive influxes of capital mostly because of jingoistic fears. American corporations may be at a disadvantage as a result of this hyperscrutiny. Setting aside the hubris of nationalism, SWFs often look for more medium or long-term investment returns than other investors, thus creating less volatility in the marketplace. Many companies can expect to have a SWF shareholder in their investor club as cross-border investments accelerate.

Sovereign Funds in Action

To help illustrate the increasing role sovereign funds are playing in the interconnected economy, reference this snapshot of investments made by such funds in U.S.-based companies and banks in the fall of 2007 alone:

- Borse Dubai, the government-controlled exchange, acquired a 19.9 percent stake in the Nasdaq and acquired the Nasdaq's 28 percent share of the London Stock Exchange.
- Mubadala Development Company, an investment arm of the Abu Dhabi government, acquired a 7.5 percent stake in the Carlyle Group for $1.35 billion.
- Citic Securities, a state-controlled Chinese investment bank, invested $1 billion in Bear Stearns before it collapsed.
- Dubai International Capital made a $1.26 billion investment in hedge fund, the Och-Ziff Capital Management Group.
- The Mubadala Development Company of Abu Dhabi strikes again, this time spending $622 million to acquire an 8 percent stake in chipmaker, Advanced Micro Devices (AMD).
- The Abu Dhabi Investment Authority, the government's sovereign wealth fund, bought a 4.9 percent stake in Citigroup for $7.5 billion.
- The China Investment Corporation, the investment arm of the Chinese government, spent $5.579 billion to acquire a 9.9 percent stake in Morgan Stanley.
- Temasek Holdings, a fund owned by the Singapore government, invested $4.4 billion to purchase a 9.4 percent interest in Merrill Lynch.[28]

The resulting criticism was arguably overblown and could have been avoided with a bit more flexibility on both sides. As Peter Weinberg, former CEO of Goldman Sachs International writes:

"Critics of SWFs often state that government investors have different constituencies, different objectives and play by different rules—and to some extent, that is true. There may be sectors where investments may not be appropriate but these should be the exception. SWFs that invest in the west must have a positive relationship with the host government. In addition, SWFs do need to demonstrate, over time, more transparency and reciprocal investing privileges."[29]

One of the obvious implications of secrecy on the part of an SWF is that it could use its financial power to attain political or economic goals like acquiring the rights to scarce resources or technologies. It is incumbent on today's global leaders, therefore, to keep a strong balance sheet in order to work with these SWFs. From a position of cash flow strength, a company's management has better leverage to negotiate with SWF leaders. If a company were desperate for funds, gaining contractual agreement and understanding of the SWF's intentions would help alleviate the fears that the investment is the beginning of a stealth takeover.

The government of Abu Dhabi, which currently has the largest SWF in terms of assets, has been moving aggressively to demonstrate the positive aspects of its investments in developed economies like the United States. The Abu Dhabi government went so far as to send a three-page letter to Henry Paulson, the U.S. Treasury Secretary, and to finance ministers at the International Monetary Fund, the World Bank, and the European Commission in which it pledged never to use its investment capital to further its political gains.[30] As Yousef al Otaiba, the nation's director of international affairs, wrote: "The benefits of Abu Dhabi's approach to international investing have been widespread—not just delivering returns to the Emirate, but also to the global economy by providing increased market liquidity, injecting capital for growth, expanding market access, creating jobs and encouraging a common global interest and commitment to mutual prosperity and prudent regulation."[31] Similarly, the government of Saudi Arabia launched a SWF in 2008 with the promise to follow the example set by the Global Pension Fund, the Norwegian SWF, which is valued for its transparency.[32]

American companies may welcome SWF investment because SWFs tend to be longer-term investors. As Aaron Bernstein writes, "Boards at many companies are likely to find [SWFs] to be a new source of patient capital that is a lot less demanding than an activist shareholder."[33] In making an investment in a company, a SWF typically plans on holding that asset rather than trading it. By trading the asset, the nation behind that SWF would inevitably face political pressure and criticism. When this fact is taken into context, a controller of a SWF can make a valuable shareholder in an organization because its investor and investee interests are often aligned both in the short and long terms. The same cannot be said of other kinds of investors who take a much more objective and shorter-term view of an asset's value.

Institutional Funds

Today's leaders confront a challenge in connecting with shareholders in the form of private equity, pension, and hedge funds, which, as a whole, are estimated to have about double the financial assets of the world's SWFs.[34] As John Bogle, the former CEO and founder of Vanguard, the low-cost mutual fund with over $100 billion in managed assets in over 80 countries, points out in his book, *The Soul of Capitalism*, the core of ownership has been flipped on its head over the past 50 years during which time direct ownership has been almost completely diluted. Institutional firms now own some 66 percent of all stock—leaving only 34 percent of all corporations directly owned.[35] The challenge this causes is that these investors do not have the mindset of an owner—they think like traders. That means that any sense of permanence or reliability is completely eroded. As Bogle describes it, "a gradual move from *owners' capitalism*—providing the lion's share of the rewards of investment to those who put up the money and risk their own capital—has culminated in an extreme version of managers' capitalism—providing vastly disproportionate rewards to those whom we have trusted to manage our enterprises in their interest of their owners."[36]

American corporate law requires a company to listen to its shareholders first and foremost. The problem is that if an organization's shareholders possess a trading mindset and, consequently, set goals driven by those things that are easily measured monthly or quarterly—such as earnings, market share, productivity, efficiency, product quality, and costs—then a short-minded view takes hold. As Bogle writes, "When measures become objectives, they are often counterproductive and self-defeating—at times producing the very results that companies wished to avoid."[37] This is analogous to the decline in U.S. high school education as the metrics used for success are now Standards of Learning test results rather than cognitive and creative learning aptitudes. While not every organization has a choice, it is clear from Bogle's arguments that public company leaders need to balance the long-term with the short-term initiatives and strive to attract shareholders that think like owners rather than traders.

As the global financial markets continue to evolve, it should prove to be interesting how the trader mindset begins to contrast with the longer-term ownership view held by many SWFs. Leaders will need to learn to account for both of these perspectives as they push their organizations forward. The power of ample communication—working to make sure that the organization clearly states its goals with its shareholders—is a great way to begin. Just as nations used to send out emissaries to scout out new trading partners and bring back news from the outside world, today's leaders need to continue to acquire and pull in information from their organization's nodes throughout the world. Recognizing the fast pace of change and quick flow of information, leaders need to convey any material shifts swiftly to their shareholders.

Venturing Ahead

Today's leader must recognize the evolving role that different shareholders play within the global economy. The challenge for leaders from countries like the United States and Japan is that, historically, neither country has a tradition of trade like that of the British, the Dutch, or the Chinese. Both American and Japanese cultures have emphasized a more isolationist and self-sufficient mindset. But the advent of globalization is like a tide that cannot be turned back—just as the legendary King Canute so visually communicated to his citizens. He wanted to prove to his people how *little* power he had. "Canute had learned that his flattering courtiers claimed he was 'So great, he could command the tides of the sea to go back.' Now Canute was not only a religious man, but also a clever politician. He knew his limitations—even if his courtiers did not—so he had his throne carried to the seashore and sat on it as the tide came in, commanding the waves to advance no further. When they didn't, he had made his point that, though the deeds of kings might appear 'great' in the minds of men, they were as nothing in the face of God's power."[38] No one man changes the results of demographics or natural law.

Once leaders from all cultures understand that the interconnected global economy is here to stay, they can begin educating both themselves and their shareholders about the critical importance of making the necessary investments to thrive in this new reality. As economist Martin Wolf in his blog responds to William Buiter, professor of European Political Economy at the London School of Economics and Political Science:

> As William Buiter has pointed out, nothing can be done to halt the diffusion of "knowledge, skills, technology, management systems" and so forth. Or at least nothing rational or decent can be done. Of course, the United States could launch an unprovoked blockade or even war with China or India. To mention such ideas is to reveal their strategic and moral bankruptcy. The United States could, it is true, try to halt the flow of ideas. The United Kingdom tried to halt the spread of technology to the United States in the early nineteenth century: it failed. The Chinese empire once made it a capital crime to export silkworms: that failed too. Similarly, protectionism against the emerging countries might slow their growth, but not halt it. Yet it would guarantee a breakdown in international relations that threatened the hopes of a peaceful future.... Everybody should

remember, above all, that the opening of the world economy is the
west's greatest economic policy achievement. It would be a tragedy if
it were to turn its back on the world just as the rest of humanity is
turning toward it.[39]

Leaders cannot fear foreign money and erect new barriers to
the free flow of those important sources of capital. Isolationism is
not an answer; staying competitive and making informed choices
is. Leaders must recognize the rapid pace of change in where the
sources of new capital are and who owns them. There is urgency
because the window of opportunity to invest is open now.

Key Points to Consider

- How do you communicate with the top shareholders in your organization? Have you learned about their motivations and time horizon in taking a stake in your company?

- As a leader in your organization, what can you do to overcome the internal tensions created by the interconnected economy?

- What opportunities can your organization explore to attract new sources of capital from emerging markets?

- Is there a bias against the role of SWFs in your organization? If so, what are the first steps you can take to give your organization some objective facts about the important role these new sources of capital can play?

- Inject urgency and pace into strategy setting and execution so you can control your own destiny. Even the largest firms have experienced a capital crunch.

The Next Stop

Now that we have a better sense of who the shareholders are in the interconnected economy, as well as what their motivations might be, it is time to continue our journey. Our next stop is to examine the role of innovation and entrepreneurs in driving momentum and change.

CHAPTER
8

Entrepreneurs from A to Z

The best way to predict the future is to invent it.

—Peter Drucker[1]

One of the purposes of this book is to encourage Westerners, and Americans in particular, to embrace the new globalization joyfully. The world is brimming with entrepreneurial talent and ambition that builds on capitalistic theories—both in developed and emerging markets, from Albania to Zimbabwe. It may not often look the same as what we see here in the United States, but we must look beyond the fringe differences to the similarities at the core. Ironically, many emerging economies are embracing the notion of open markets and innovation in an effort to catch up at a time when many of their Western counterparts find themselves embroiled in the notion of protectionist policies. Global leaders must overcome their preconceived notions that capitalism thrives only in Western countries to tap into the burgeoning number of motivated and talented people that are shaking the globe in emerging markets not only through innovative new products, but also through simple hard work, efficiency, and expertise.

Leaders of developing countries are making decisions that they hope will benefit their own people. In many instances, these decisions employ a tentative reliance on free markets as a means of improving living standards, but with a protectionist or supportive government role that recognizes the fragility of the developing nation's economy. One example is Muhammad Yunus, founder of Grameen Bank and winner of the Nobel Prize in 2006 for his efforts at creating micro-credit for poor people without any financial security in developing economies like Bangladesh. Or consider the nation of Malawi in Africa, which said "no thanks" to loans offered by the World Bank, and instead developed a thriving agricultural economy on its own by promoting deep fertilizer subsidies.[2] While neither of these stories may fit the strict definition of free market capitalism, each provides an example of entrepreneurial innovation and an embracing of the market. These steps should be applauded for signaling the direction in which their countries are headed.

Entrepreneurship may be the most dynamic factor in improving the economies of developing nations. The term *entrepreneur* often means different things to different people. But in our context, let's start with the dictionary definition: "A person who organizes and manages any enterprise, especially a business, usually with considerable initiative and risk."[3] Said in a different way, entrepreneurs are those among us that have the passion and the energy to convert ideas into action and thereby bring results that benefit more than just the entrepreneur. But entrepreneurs and the benefits they bring are not always understood. As John Willman of the *Financial Times* wrote: "Entrepreneurs have often been seen by their contemporaries as unreasonable. Think of Henry Ford, paying his workers twice the going rate to mass produce identical black cars by the million. Or the pioneers behind low-cost airlines such as Southwest Airlines and Ryanair who launched discount flights with none of the frills offered by traditional carriers. Or Sir James Dyson, inventor of the bagless vacuum cleaner, who had to create his own company to make it."[4]

The influence of entrepreneurs can be understood by looking at results in five categories:[5]

1. *Developing new markets:* Since entrepreneurs are sensitive to the needs of consumers, they have the incentive to branch into new markets to supply those needs.

2. *Discovering new sources of materials:* Because entrepreneurs operate under the laws of supply and demand, they are constantly looking for ways to get either cheaper or better supplies to meet the demand of their customers.

3. *Mobilizing capital resources:* Entrepreneurs are like cooks in that they turn sources of capital, like money and labor, into goods and services.

4. *Introducing new technologies:* In their unending effort to supply the market's needs, entrepreneurs are often at the forefront of developing new technologies both to cut costs and to create new products.

5. *Creating employment:* One of the most critical contributions entrepreneurs add to any society is their ability to create jobs—the lifeblood of consumer markets and governments alike.

Entrepreneurs can be found in all kinds of organizations: large and small, mature and startup, profit and not-for-profit. In short, entrepreneurs are individuals who embrace the capitalistic system of risks and rewards to bet their own personal capital in the pursuit of profit through innovative products and services. As Peter Drucker once wrote, to be capable of innovating, a business or organization "has to make sure its incentives, compensation, personnel decisions, and policies all reward the right entrepreneurial behavior and do not penalize it."[6] Doing so will literally open an entire new world of possibilities. Charles Handy writes in his book *The Elephant and the Flea:* "I have little doubt that capitalism breeds innovation. Without the chance to turn ideas into profits, many of those ideas would languish in the minds of the individuals who thought of them. Many scientific breakthroughs would still be left in the laboratories of the institutes and universities where they were made, recorded only in the pages of scientific journals. More people are healthier, live longer and more comfortably (except in parts of Russia and Africa), can do more, go to more places and enjoy more options for their lives, because of capitalism."[7]

Adam Smith is a Scottish philosopher who is often acknowledged as the father of economics. While Smith is better known as the author of *The Wealth of Nations*, he first wrote about the greater good that results when people pursue their personal interests. In *The Theory of Moral Sentiments*, first published in 1759, Smith wrote about his notion of the "invisible hand": "In spite of their natural selfishness and rapacity, though they mean only their own convenience, though the sole end which they propose . . . be the gratification of their own vain and insatiable desires, they divide with the poor the produce of all their improvements. They are led by an invisible hand to make nearly the same distribution of the necessaries of life, which would have been made, had the earth been divided into equal portions among all its inhabitants, and thus without intending it, without knowing it, advance the interest of the society."[8]

When the "invisible hand" of the market sets entrepreneurs loose to create innovative products and services, society as a whole benefits. This rule of social organization applies just as well in developing, emerging markets as in developed ones.

Disaggregation Leads to Innovation

The greater the competition, the more innovative each and every organization needs to be in order to stand out. Globalization brings greater competition. Innovation is required more than ever because customers have an ever-growing list of options from which to buy products. As legendary venture capitalist John Doerr, a partner at Kleiner Perkins Caufield & Byers, has said: "Innovation is a win-win game. It makes the whole world more prosperous."[9] When individuals are given the incentive to innovate—by receiving some form of compensation for their work—great things result. Part of courageous leadership, therefore, involves a willingness to empower people who may appear to lack the education, training, or experience to act on their own initiatives. The key to succeeding in a global market, therefore, is to enable your employees to lead you to the new ideas that will set your organization apart from the competition. To do this, leaders need to focus on creating an organizational structure that takes advantage of different global perspectives. Nontraditional managerial talent from across the globe, including women and young people from developing nations, may be uniquely capable of offering the desired new perspectives. Exposure to a diverse group of individuals and their ideas fosters integrative thinking. A.G. Lafley, the head of Procter & Gamble since 2000, defines integrative thinking as the ability to consider various points of view of a consumer, the market segment, system costs, and the context of competition and find a way to develop a unique business model. He quotes Roger Martin, dean of the Rotman School of Management at the University of Toronto: "An integrative thinker finds unobvious connections and patterns from a diverse set of factors. They [sic] see more things as relevant and important, such as contradictions in what customers say and what they actually do. They then bring it all together by synthesizing and translating salient information into simple insights that lead to action. Integrative thinkers are creative problem solvers because they find solutions to break the tensions of opposing ideas."[10]

Lafley develops the notion that true breakthrough innovations occur not in silos, but in open environments in which new opportunities are uncovered through simultaneous consideration of seemingly disparate elements. We are now witnessing this very principle at work among many successful multinational companies, like Procter & Gamble (P&G), that have basically disaggregated their research and development operations around the world to take advantage of market-specific insights and pools of entrepreneurial talent. Dr. Rolf-Christian Wentz, a lecturer on innovation and marketing at the University of Hamburg, has studied how organizations like P&G, Toyota, GE, 3M, IBM, Google, Microsoft, Sony, Hewlett-Packard, DuPont, Honeywell, and Whirlpool have changed the structure of their organizations to spur the rate at which innovation and new ideas are generated. P&G has been particularly innovative, he writes in his book, *The Innovation Machine*, because it has embraced a concept known as "open innovation":

> *Open Innovation is a core strategy of innovation management in order to get innovations to market more rapidly and enable Fast Innovation. In order to execute Open Innovation and to channel external solutions and ideas into the company, innovation management needs an effective external interface. For this purpose P&G has established its External Business Development Organization and its Connect & Develop Organization. The Mission of these departments is to realize the innovation potential, which slumbers in the outside world, via the development of external networks. Not the least because of its Open Innovation P&G has dramatically increased its innovation speed. An innovation which in the past would have taken three years or more to get to market these days can be rolled-out globally within 18 months.*[11]

Large companies frequently have the resources to implement innovative ideas like Open Innovation, but sometimes their reliance on traditional business structures limits the opportunity for new ideas to percolate to management's awareness. As a result, corporations have employed a process of decentralization over the last 15 to 20 years, as a means of encouraging entrepreneurship and individual employee responsibility within large organizations. The need for decentralization may be greatest in multinational businesses in which decision making must be driven by an awareness of multiple cultural, economic, and political factors in various nations. Indigenous people provide important insights to Western countries doing business in their lands, but only if they are empowered to act.

As Satish Nambisan and Mohanbir Sawhney write in their book, *The Global Brain*, we are seeing more and more companies adopting a platform of "global network-centric innovation."[12] With global R&D increasingly moving to places like India and China, as Figure 8.1 illustrates, companies are adapting both by opening their own R&D centers in these emerging markets and by

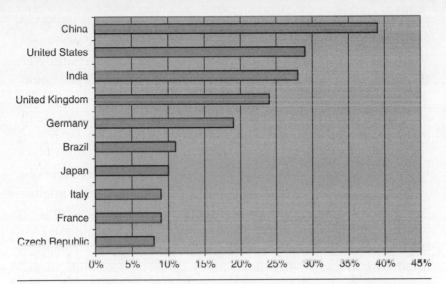

Figure 8.1 The New Centers for Research and Development (R&D Spending 2004–2007). *Data source:* Accenture, Economist Intelligence Unit, "Scattering the Seeds of Invention: The Globalization of Research and Development," 2004.

seeking out partnerships with other organizations around the world so that they may be able to complement each other's strengths. In his book, *Flight of the Creative Class*, economist Richard Florida researched global patent filings and found that different geographic areas tended to specialize in certain technologies. U.S. companies, for instance, lead in filing patents for high-tech fields like computers, software and multicellular organisms and also areas like "wells" and "earth-penetrating apparatus." Japanese patents also covered high-tech areas like photography, photocopying and optical systems, while German patents tended to be focused on automotive technologies, advanced materials and manufacturing technologies.[13] By decentralizing their source for new ideas, therefore, organizations can also remain nimble enough to take advantage of new ideas regardless of where they originate.

Consider the example of the Haier Electronics Group, with headquarters in Qingdao, Shangdong Province, China, which manufactures washing machines and water heaters and is the fourth largest white goods home appliance manufacturer in the world. While Westerners may think that most washing machines have the same basic and boxy design, Haier has created many models, such as a telescope appearance with bionic modern design and smart technology. Haier has been able to take a commanding lead in the global market for washing machines by relying on innovation to adapt its products to different markets. Haier has obtained more than 7,000 patented technology certifications, including 1,234 for Haier inventions and 589 software intellectual property rights in its efforts to create a world-class company in the fields of home integration, network appliances, digital and large-scale integrated circuits, and new materials. As the company celebrated its twenty-first anniversary at the end of 2005, it also announced the fourth leg of its strategy—global brand building, extending the brand building, diversification, and globalization strategies of its early company life cycle. To that end, and in the spirit of the global network-centric innovation, Haier has established 10 information centers and 6 design institutes in countries like China, Malaysia, and the United States to aid in the development of competitive products based on the demand of local consumers around the world.[14]

Haier's CEO, Zhang Ruimin, is also attuned to opportunities that might unexpectedly present themselves. When Haier began selling its washing machines into rural China, complaints of defective water pipes began flooding back to headquarters. When service teams went out to investigate the problem, however, they found that it wasn't a problem with the pipes as such; rather, the pipes were clogged with yam skins. The villagers apparently thought their new machines were more useful in cleaning their fruits and vegetables than in cleaning their clothes. Unlike a more stodgy mainstream company that might have dismissed the villagers outright, Ruimin employed a bit of entrepreneurial innovation and integrative reasoning to come up with a different solution. He set his R&D team to work designing a new machine with wider pipes that could both clean clothes and large root vegetables like yams. And so, Haier's

Big Yam washing machine was born—and it has been a bestseller ever since.[15]

Identifying New Opportunities

Returning to one of the themes of this book—namely the power that measuring brings to decision makers—let us look further into the ways we can measure innovation or at least map out ways that we can appreciate the impact that new products and services can have on both existing and developing markets. Perhaps you've heard about recent market struggles like "the browser wars," which pitted Microsoft's Internet Explorer against Netscape's Navigator[16] or even the HD-DVD versus Blu-Ray war fought over the standard format for DVD movies.[17] But did you ever hear about the "cheese slice wars?" When I was working at Kraft Foods in the 1980s, we were fighting a war for market share with our rival Borden in a segment of the cheese business. Our market was defined as IWPS, individually wrapped processed-cheese slices, frequently used in sandwiches. While we had the dominant position in the market with our brand Kraft Singles, Borden was continually chipping away at our lead. That's when we organized a three-day strategy session to apply the framework for competitor analysis as described in Michael Porter's classic textbook *Competitive Strategy: Techniques for Analyzing Industries and Competitors.* Porter, a professor at Harvard Business School, developed a system for the structural analysis of industries, as shown in Figure 8.2, in 1979.[18]

At the time, the Kraft Singles brand was a $400 million business unit at Kraft. At that level of sales revenue, this product was as large as a Fortune 500 company. Our market shares varied, but had dropped as much as 800 basis points in some markets. Each market had different dynamics for this significant change. Sometimes the consumer promotions from Borden entered the market before ours, creating an incentive for the consumer to switch to their brand. Sometimes, the retailers had received special deals from Borden to stock and display their product before we had made our best offer.

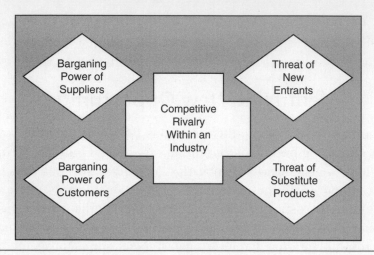

Figure 8.2   Porter's Five Broad Competitive Forces. Adapted from Michael Porter, *Competitive Strategy: Techniques for Analyzing Industries and Competitors* (New York: Free Press, 1980), p. 4.

By applying the Five Forces model—the bargaining power of buyers and sellers, the threat of new entrants and substitute products, and the competition with existing rivals—we were able to put together a strategic plan to increase sales, reverse the gains of the Borden's IWPS brand, and regain our lost market share. Each city and situation required special attention so we knew which threat to combat. What makes Porter's Five Forces model so attractive is it boils the essence of capitalism down to its very roots. By using these forces to construct a picture of a market, a company or an organization can devise the means to either attack or defend the opportunities that market presents. The Five Forces have utility beyond Fortune 500 companies. If you use Porter's model as a map, it can help you begin to notice how innovative capitalism permeates the globe—often in places where you might least expect it. As an example of this, consider the story of an innovative organization in Mumbai, India.

If you were to look up innovative entrepreneurs in a dictionary, you just might find a picture of a *dabbawalla*, a Hindi word that literally translates as one who carries a box. It is often used to describe someone who is employed in a unique service industry built around the delivery of home-cooked lunches to office workers in Mumbai. Dressed in white garb, these workers carry boxes constructed of wood and metal several feet long above their heads, transporting dozens of lunches at a time. Originally conceived in 1880 as a means of supplying British nationals with the foods of their choice, the system has evolved to meet the needs of the modern Indian professional. Today, the system operates as a charitable trust under the name Mumbai Tiffin Box Carriers Association, and it is as deceptively simple as it is ingenuous.[19]

Commuting in Mumbai is a nightmare. A dense population of 25 million residents and streets crowded with vehicles of all kinds make going home for lunch or even out to a restaurant impossible for most of the city's workers. Further, many workers simply cannot afford to buy their lunches on a daily basis. The *dabbawallas* provide approximately 200,000 workers with freshly cooked meals delivered to their offices every work day for about 300 rupees (U.S. $7) a month.[20] Here's how the system works:

1. The first dabbawalla picks up the box, or *dabba*, containing the day's meal from a home and takes it to the nearest railway station.

2. The second *dabbawalla* sorts out the *dabbas* at the railway station according to their intended destinations and then puts them in the appropriate luggage carriages on a train.

3. The third *dabbawalla* travels with the *dabbas* to the railway stations nearest to the destinations.

4. The fourth deliveryman picks up the *dabbas* from the railway station and delivers them to each individual's office.

5. The process is reversed in the evenings, with each *dabba* returning to its home. Each box changes hands about eight times during the day and the average distance traveled is about 70 kilometers or 40 miles every day.

To make this seemingly unprofitable arrangement work, the *dabbawallas* employ a sophisticated and widespread distribution organization throughout the city that connects everyone from those that cook the food to those that pick up and deliver it using various cars, trains, and bicycles as transportation that employs an estimated 4,500 to 5,000 deliverymen, each of whom makes the exact same wage—something in the range of about $123 a month.[21] The *dabbawalla*'s organization proves that the "invisible hand" of capitalism takes on many different forms. In this case, the organization results in a win-win situation for everyone involved and the industry continues to grow about 20 percent a year.

But as innovative as the *dabbawalla* organization is, it is also sensitive to the notion that competition can emerge from anywhere. That's why the *dabbawallas* agreed to subject their business model for examination under the Porter's Five Forces framework to determine their competitive position in Mumbai's food delivery economy. In their analysis, they found the following:

1. *Competition:* Due to the organization's widespread distribution system, new entrants would be hard pressed to match the efficiency of the *dabbawallas.*

2. *New entrants:* Due to its exploding population, Mumbai has been inundated with both fast-food establishments and office canteens. Since neither serves home-cooked meals, however, the *dabbawallas* can maintain their competitive differential.

3. *Bargaining power of buyers:* Since delivery rates are so low already, buyers have little incentive to try and negotiate lower prices.

4. *Bargaining power of sellers:* Since the organization relies on its own members to do everything from cook to deliver lunches, there are few suppliers with whom to bargain.

5. *Threat of a new substitute product or service:* With their organization in place, it's hard to imagine a new competitor in the home-cooked lunch delivery service emerging in the foreseeable future.

Any organization looking to make inroads into the Indian consumer economy would greatly benefit from studying how the

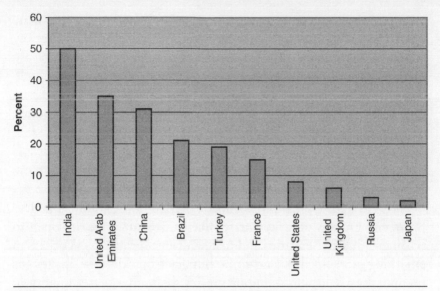

Figure 8.3 Global Entrepreneurial Ambition. Adapted from *Global Entrepreneurship Monitor, 2007 Executive Report*, www.gemconsortium.org/download.asp?fid=644/.

dabbawallas continue to dominate their respective market. But India is far from the only emerging market that harbors entrepreneurial intentions. In fact, residents of emerging markets often have greater entrepreneurial ambitions than their peers in the West. As Figure 8.3 illustrates, an annual study conducted in 2007 by Babson College and the London Business School called the Global Entrepreneurship Monitor found that the residents of countries like India, United Arabs Emirates, China, and Brazil are more likely to strike out on entrepreneurial ventures than residents of France, Japan, and even the United States—the supposed home of entrepreneurial thinking.

Accessing Human Capital

Entrepreneurs must have access to capital to pursue their visions. This is the basic premise behind the capitalist system. When entrepreneurs have free access to capital, innovation happens. As we discussed in Chapter 7, emerging markets are becoming key suppliers of capital to the interconnected economy. But there are several kinds of capital. Entrepreneurs need both monetary capital, as well as human resource capital. In other words, in order to bring about innovation through action in the interconnected economy, entrepreneurs need access to talented employees in many different markets.

Countries like France that do not encourage their innovators through tax incentives or public policies may inadvertently push innovators to seek opportunities outside of their home country. Unlike Japan and France, other countries like India and China are open to trading with other cultures and fostering entrepreneurs. Workers in emerging markets also tend to be hungry to tackle new challenges because they see them as opportunities to attain a better quality of life than their parents or grandparents may have experienced. As one young worker from India explained, Westerners who talk about work/life balance are missing out. "The West likes life, we like to work," he said. That means that if the current policies in your home country are not creating sufficient growth, employment, and stability, you must look elsewhere—and it is in the emerging markets that are increasingly opening up and removing their own barriers where you may find it. The competitive pace is quickening around the globe and the countries that create barriers for innovation and entrepreneurial talent will lose out.

The challenge for global leaders, then, is both to tap into the best markets for talent and to develop it where they need it. Getting access to the right kind of human capital is a critical element to any entrepreneurial success. In earlier chapters, I noted how the education and training for young people in developing markets is, in many cases, superior to that received by young people in the United States. The difference is magnified when factors such a willingness to work hard and an entrepreneurial spirit, including a disposition to risk taking, are factored in. Increasingly, Western businesses will look to foreign workers. Often this requires business leaders to overcome cultural barriers, including those built around national borders. Western nations have been overly protective of domestic laborers. Consider the example of two different "island" nations: Denmark and Singapore.

Denmark, on one hand, has one of the highest activity rates in the world among men and women in its labor force. With a population of 5.4 million people, according to *Eurostat*, the statistical office of the E.U., 74.3 percent of the nation's women and 81.2 percent of its men are active participants in the Danish economy, which results in an unemployment rate of about 3.8 percent, one of the lowest in the E.U. But Danish companies can only fulfill 60 percent of their orders because they simply don't have enough human capital to increase their production. According to Mark Spelman from Accenture, even though Denmark is at 97 percent employment, cultural resistance and protectionist attitudes keep the nation's economy closed to new sources of talent. Many Danes are aware of this dilemma and are now working to remedy the situation through awareness programs and education. Denmark has high levels of lifelong learning with nearly 80 percent of adults aged 15 to 64 participating in some form of learning activity. This is the third highest in the EU 15 (behind Austria and Luxembourg).

Singapore, on the other hand, faces a similar talent shortage among its native population of 4.5 million people, but it has gone about solving its problem in a very different manner. In attempting to fulfill its goal of becoming the world's financial hub, Singapore has opened the doors to its economy to comers of any national origin or culture—if someone has the talent, he or she is welcome to ply a trade in the free market. The Singapore Economic Development Board estimates that of the 7,000 or so multinationals in Singapore today, about two thirds are managing regional responsibilities out of Singapore. The list of companies with regional headquarters in Singapore includes, among others, Microsoft, Merck, and Lenovo. Singapore has been investing in education for its girls and boys and adults for decades. Now the country is reaping the benefits. The country ranks first (tied with Finland) for the quality of its education system and first (tied with Belgium) in terms of the quality of math and science education in schools, per the WEF report 2007–2008.[22]

If you doubted which policy decision was more effective, we can simply turn to the financial results for the answer. Since 2003, Denmark's GDP has grown, on average, 2.1 percent per year whereas Singapore has enjoyed GDP growth of 7.1 percent per year over the same time period.[23]

Research supports the fact that immigrants often make the best entrepreneurs. In his book *The Hypomanic Edge*, John D. Gartner, a clinical assistant professor of psychiatry at Johns Hopkins University Medical School, writes about the common personality traits—a seemingly boundless energy to create and explore—shared by both immigrants and entrepreneurs. As he writes: "Successful entrepreneurs are not just braggarts. They are highly creative people who quickly generate a tremendous number of ideas—some clever, others ridiculous. Their 'flight of ideas,' jumping from topic to topic in a rapid energized way, is a sign of hypomania."[24]

By the same definition, Gartner writes: "Hypomanics are ideally suited by temperament to become immigrants. If you are an impulsive, optimistic, high-energy risk taker, you are more likely to undertake a project that requires a lot of energy, entails a lot of risk, and might seem daunting if you thought about it too much."[25]

In summary, Gartner credits much of the economic success of the United States over the past two centuries to its largely immigrant population. The lesson learned is that protectionist policies toward immigration turn off the spigot to an influx of entrepreneurial talent and innovation. Even those supposedly "protected" will suffer as a result. Instead of creating unintended consequences, consider leveraging the facts to your advantage.

Opportunities to serve the immigrant population abound. The CEO of Western Union, Christina A. Gold, observes how her company capitalizes on the global migration. "There are over 200 million people today who live in countries other than the country of their birth. We monitor 15,000 to 20,000 corridors, and we connect the migrants of the world as they move and want to send money back home. Now, 65 percent of our business is not in the United States. If you look at our business six years ago, we had 100,000 locations; now we have 345,000 globally. We're talking about people in

China, southern India. They are going to the Middle East to work to feed their families."[26] If the company's leaders had not changed the strategy from delivering telegrams to delivering money, it would not exist today. In fact, after 145 years, on January 27, 2006, the company discontinued all telegram and commercial messaging services so it could focus on connecting people by sending money.

Opportunity Begins at Home

When politicians and pundits, playing off the fears of many Americans, argue for protectionism and closing the doors to new immigrants, I shudder. What has made the United States as strong as it is has been the embracing of personal freedoms and open markets, in comparison to many countries. The experiences of past immigrants help to put this point in perspective. For example, Carlos Gutierrez, U.S. Secretary of Commerce, and Arnold Schwarzenegger, the governor of California, co-authored an article in the *Wall Street Journal* in May 2008 that argued for keeping America open to free trade. As they wrote: "For all the openness to trade and investment, it is America's openness to people that is the indispensable factor in our growth. Each of us knows that well. While we need to secure borders, we also need to develop a sensible, comprehensive immigration policy that is humane, practical and consistent with the spirit of openness that is our nation's strength."[27]

Consider also the story of Joaquin Fraga, an owner and operator based in Jacksonville, Florida, who drives for the global leader of executive limousine companies, Carey International, Inc. I had the opportunity to hear Joaquin's personal story about escaping from Cuba and it really struck me. His mother's sister was an entertainer and happened to be performing in Mexico when Castro led the revolution in Cuba. She sought asylum in the United States and requested that her extended family join her. But the response to the requests didn't happen fast enough, and that's when Castro's government came down hard on Joaquin's family.

"My father ran a nightclub and restaurant which the government took over to prevent us from having money to pay to leave the country. A month later, there was a knock on my parent's front door. The soldier told us to take whatever we could carry. They told us that we were being evicted from our home. For the next five years, we lived in a small apartment in Havana. I had one piece of bread and a cube of sugar with water for breakfast. No lunch. For dinner, I had rice and one egg each night. I was always hungry. I had no shoes and one set of clothes." At that time, in 1961, he was nine years old. After five years of living in total poverty, his family finally emigrated to Miami.

I met Joaquin when he was 56 years old, a former green beret, a limo driver, and a husband for 34 years. He told me there is no greater country than the United States. When I asked why, he said, "It is the only place that provides opportunity to reach your dreams." He traveled and lived in many places as a member of the U.S. Army. He told me that in Amsterdam and in U.S. cities he saw how diverse people work together, and that this diversity seemingly compelled all to work hard. I asked what his most difficult Green Beret experience was. He said going into Colombia to perform contra-narcotic actions and deal with the corruption. He and his team were ambushed because some local citizens in the chain took bribes and revealed the covert action. Several people died.

The lesson learned from our conversations was that while the United States does indeed have some problems, we need the talent that immigrants bring to a society. We need the loyalty they give to a country that provided them a chance to create dreams and then fulfill them. To hear Joaquin describe his arrival at Miami airport, which used to have something called the Freedom House to welcome new immigrants, you can literally feel his passion for his adopted country. He describes the tables of food offered to him, the pile of donated clothes from which he could choose new outfits and sneakers—his first pair in his life. He smiles as he describes his first sight after the plane landed—a blonde blue-eyed stewardess beckoning him to come off the plane, telling him that he was finally safe.

Joaquin is a global citizen and he would never want to live anywhere other than the United States. He used the future tense saying, "We will have many opportunities if we work and learn. I am glad to fight for and go into combat for this country, knowing my buddy's head might be shot off and land on my shoulder. We fight to protect our buddies."

Breeding Entrepreneurs

Leaders must first make the most out of the resources they are given to venture out—both in the context of national borders as well as the walls of an organization. That means leaders need to cultivate an entrepreneurial atmosphere within their organizations that encourages older workers to revitalize their skills and to learn new ones. Younger workers, as we discussed in Chapter 5, will also thrive when leaders engage them with tasks that result in turning new ideas and technologies into actions. Just like with any form of capital, there is an urgent need to develop an entrepreneurial mindset within and outside multinationals. New ideas originate from employees that lead to innovation. The entrepreneurial spirit resides in people, regardless of whether they are employed in their own firm, a small organization, or a large multinational.

The challenge for leaders is this: the realities of the interconnected economy dictate that in order not only to survive but also to thrive, organizations need to innovate. But to generate the kinds of new ideas and hard work that lead to innovation, organizations need to tap the best sources of entrepreneurial spirit, which are often in emerging markets. That means organizations not only need to go global, they may need to break themselves down into smaller components based around the world to take advantage of different talent pools and to get firsthand research on how they need to change their products and services to meet global appetites.

Bulldozing Barriers

To do business in various countries, and tap into its potential stores of entrepreneurial innovation, courageous leaders need to embrace and adapt to the realities of a particular country's culture. Japan, for instance, as Figure 8.3 demonstrates, is probably one of the least likely countries to foster entrepreneurs. There, the "company man" has been the model of business success for many decades. Entrepreneurs, like the founders of Honda and Sony, are hard to come by. In recognition of this point, a Japanese newspaper from 2002 printed the following question: "In the Japan that has for a long time been called 'the barren land of entrepreneurs,' various efforts are being undertaken. Will entrepreneurial spirit be able to take root in the Japanese economy?"[28]

I personally encountered the differences in encouraging entrepreneurism between the United States and Japan when I was hiring a chief financial officer for a newly established Sara Lee office in Tokyo. It seemed odd that the only resumes I received from the search firm were for candidates who came from Mars, Coca-Cola, Johnson & Johnson, and other American-based companies. So I asked to see some people who had developed their careers in Japanese companies. After some tittering, the recruiter said I would never be able to hire someone like that. Naively, I asked, "Why not?" He said that once a man starts at a Japanese company, he stays with it until he retires. "Anyone who has been contaminated by foreign ideas and who has worked in a different pace and culture would be rejected by the antibodies of a Japanese firm," he told me. No self-respecting Japanese man would take the risk to work for a foreign firm for fear of being blocked from returning to his planned and predictable career ladder leading up through the Japanese company. That meant, of course, that only those employees who worked for non-Japanese companies would be interested in interviewing and competing for a position at an American company such as that for which I worked. I learned an important lesson that day: It takes a courageous leader or a crisis to breach tradition in a closed society.

This protectionist or paternalistic attitude fostered the development of additional walls or barriers between employees and employers. Even today Japan continues to struggle as it attempts to tap into new labor pools. Facing a severe nursing shortage, for instance, Japan has turned to neighboring countries like Indonesia, Thailand, and the Philippines for trainees. But rather than opening its labor market, Japan continues to enforce severe restrictions on these imported workers, requiring six months of Japanese language training, three to four years of medical training, and even a competency test before the workers are allowed to remain in the country.[29] The Japanese mindset, it could be said, would sound something like "unless you have something to offer us, we don't want anything to do with you." Obviously, even if an entrepreneur saw an opportunity to supply nurses to the Japanese market, he or she would first have to overcome some significant cultural and political barriers.

Another example of a national economy that risks falling behind is France. French culture celebrates government service over entrepreneurship. As the French historian and economist Nicholas Baverez wrote: "Suffice it to say that France is the only developed country where the average remuneration of government workers exceeds that of private sector employees by 11 percent and where the average income of retirees exceeds that of active workers by 10 percent."[30] As a result of small business obstacles, France ranks in the top 10 countries in terms of regulatory red tape for doing business in the country as shown in Table 8.1. It is no surprise that France's best and brightest talent eagerly seek government positions for high pay, low risk. Would-be French entrepreneurs flee the country in search of more capitalist-friendly environments such as the United Kingdom, where an estimated 500,000 French men and women, most of them under the age of 35, have gone to seek their fortunes.[31] The United Kingdom is changing at a faster pace for French youth, but still has significant industrial and tax regulations.

If we turn to the results the World Economic Forum (WEF)'s 2007–2008 Global Competitive Index introduced in Chapter 1,

Table 8.1   Red Tape Rankings

Most Red Tape	Least Red Tape
Canada	Croatia
Australia	Venezuela
New Zealand	Poland
United States	Philippines
Singapore	China
Hong Kong	Ecuador
United Kingdom	Jordan
Puerto Rico	Uruguay
Ireland	Greece
France	UAE

Source: World Bank, "Doing Business,"
www.doingbusiness.org (accessed June 9, 2008).

entitled "Today's Interconnected Globe," the United States, while ranked number one in terms of its competitiveness out of 131 countries analyzed by the WEF, also has some chinks in its economic armor—high tax rates and government bureaucracy, in particular. The economy of Finland (which ranks sixth on the competitive economy index list), also struggles under high tax rates and restrictive labor and tax regulations.

The story is the same in the United Kingdom: ranked ninth, with high tax rates and regulations, but also suffers from an inadequately educated workforce for today's global economy. The lack of a skilled workforce is a common problem with both highly ranked countries like Singapore (ranked 7) as well as emerging markets like Vietnam (68). Vietnam suffers from low scores in innovation, business sophistication, and higher education, which have led to the country's overall ranking slipping four spots from 64 in 2006–2007 to 68 in 2007–2008. Efficiency of its labor market and its market size are the only marks in which the country scored in the top 50 of all countries. The implications for Vietnamese competitiveness in the future are clear. Because the economy of Vietnam is based on basic services and low-cost manufacturing, without investments in training and development of higher-skilled workers, it is less insulated from economic threats. When there is turmoil in the global economy, the country will feel it more than other countries—as the devaluation of the country's currency in June 2008 suggests. Korea provides a significant contrast in competitiveness to Vietnam. Korea earns high scores for its higher education system, technological readiness, business sophistication, and innovative abilities—all of which ranked in the top 10 of countries surveyed by the WEF. On the basis of these strengths, Korea, which ranked number 23 in overall competitiveness in 2006–2007, leapt to 11 on the 2007–2008 WEF index.

Competition can indeed come from anywhere. There are sources of information such as WEF that can supply some clues where the best of those competitors may be biding their time or new competitors will emerge. At the same time, this information can also be used to highlight the weaknesses that might exist in geographies in which your organization is already operating. When competitive comparisons reveal potential liabilities and future threats, this analysis will provide a leading indicator and impetus from which you and your organization can act.

Beware the Mirage of Open Markets

Some appearances of open markets can be deceiving. I learned this in the fall of 2006 when I visited Dubai. Just before I was to leave the country, I read a news article about how the government of Sheikh Mohammed had recently passed a law that allowed foreigners to buy homes. Up until that point, foreigners were not allowed to own any property. After reading the story, I had a chance to speak to a group of local businesspeople and I commented that it sounded as though the new law was a sign of progress, that capitalism was at work. Perhaps this new openness would help spur the country's booming economy with new entrepreneurs buying and selling houses. "Now," I said, "anyone can sell his home for a profit." "Hold on," someone in the crowd said. "The law didn't say anything about *selling* a home. For that, a foreigner would still need to seek the permission of the princes that ran the government." I learned that sometimes what looks like an open market for entrepreneurs really isn't.

Urgent Need to Act

The results of a McKinsey Global Survey published in 2008 showed that most business leaders today know that they need to expand globally.[32] At the same time, many of those same leaders fail to act—or worse, fail to respond in the manner that the new realities of the interconnected economy dictate. The longer those leaders wait, the greater the risk is that their organizations will fall behind because of the competition, especially with the increasing number of emerging market multinationals. Donald N. Sull addressed this concern when he asked a critical question in his 1999 *Harvard Business Review* article entitled, "Why Good Companies Go Bad." The central theme of Sull's piece is that successful companies that face big changes in their environment often fail to respond effectively. As he writes: "Unable to defend themselves against competitors armed with new products, technologies, or strategies, they watch their sales and profits erode, their best people leave, and their stock valuations tumble. Some ultimately recover—usually after painful rounds of downsizing and restructuring—but many don't."[33]

Sull's interesting conclusion is that previously very successful companies failed to take the appropriate action because of something he calls "active inertia," which he defines as an organization's tendency to follow established patterns of behavior. What has worked before must work now, even in confronting dramatic environmental shifts. "Stuck in the modes of thinking and working that brought success in the past, market leaders simply accelerate their tried-and-true activities. In trying to dig themselves out of a hole, they just deepen it," he writes. In other words, companies need to embrace entrepreneurial thinking and innovation in order to evolve. And the pressure to do so *now* has become intense with the advent of the interconnected economy. As Peter Drucker told me, and as Michael

Porter reinforces with the help of his strategic Five Forces model, new threats and competitors can come from literally anywhere in the global economy at any time. That means that organizations need to become more nimble in overcoming barriers in order to access new talent and sources of innovation before they too find themselves on the outside looking in.

Key Points to Consider

- Consider ways that your organization can supercharge its innovation efforts. Is there a way to empower an "invisible hand" to help out?

- Think of a first step you can take tomorrow to connect to a new talent source for your organization. How can Michael Porter's Five Forces model help your organization to assess where you can take advantage of opportunities or head off new threats and competitors?

- What is your organization doing to overcome barriers to human capital in the markets you operate in?

- If you think of your organization as disaggregated, what functions or product lines need new sources of innovation or how can you participate in Open Innovation?

- What is your organization going to do tomorrow to combat the possibility of falling into the trap of "active inertia?"

The Next Stop

As we have discussed, it is truly the world's entrepreneurs who drive innovation. But, they can't do it alone. They need to create or work for organizations that have "sticky" brands that attract new talented people. The key to motivating action is when multiple parties share the same platform, respectful of each other's goals and values. That leads us to the next stop on our journey: exploring the role of individual and organizational values in the context of a global interconnected economy.

Values and Global Context

I n Chapter 1, we discussed the fact that many Americans, along with other citizens of the developed world, fear the effects of globalization. That fear is based on the assumption that Western societies might be compelled to "regress" in some areas, such as environmental awareness, women's rights, or workplace safety, to compete better in traditional manufacturing and other labor-intensive industries. This kind of fear remains a powerful tool in slowing and combating globalization. I contend that Western social goals are best pursued through free governments and free markets. I believe that the growth of democracy and capitalism throughout the world in the twenty-first century can become the means of securing the rights to clean air, equal employment opportunity, and a safe place to work for all people.

However, to achieve this goal, Westerners will temporarily have to accept a moral relativism and work within the values and norms of the various cultures in which business is conducted. Fortunately, this moral relativism is a well-established precept of the belief system that underlies democracy and free enterprise, both of which depend on the recognition of inherent human rights. People are born equal and that equality is recognized in rights to self-determination, exercised both politically and economically. Each and every individual is recognized as having an equal right to make his or her own political and economic choices. The significance of this recognition is well explained in a story used by my husband, a legal historian. He draws the distinction between post-Revolutionary America—a time when individual rights, private autonomy, and human equality were valued—and colonial America in which hierarchal duty and Christian morality were embraced as the basis for law. The story indicates how under contract law, each person is respected as reasonable, rational, self-interested, and equal. Contract law, which also serves as the governing force for free markets, allows each individual to determine his or her own destiny without a societal imposition of values.

Assume that a wealthy farmer in 1790 was relaxing in a tavern having a beer with other local gentlemen when a poor drunk, a father of four young children, came into town leading his last cow. The cow was not a prime specimen, worth perhaps five dollars. Its owner wanted only to spend the afternoon with a bottle of whiskey, which cost two dollars. He asked the bar patrons if anyone would buy his cow. Receiving no offers, he encouraged interest by proposing the sale of the cow for only four dollars. Still there was no offer. Finally, the rich farmer, knowing the poor man's alcoholism and the price of a bottle of whiskey, offered two dollars for the cow. An agreement was reached, hands were shaken, and the money and the cow were exchanged. In the contract law of the 1790s, the agreement would be enforceable. The bargain was acceptable for having been struck between two legal equals who owed no duty to each other besides that embodied in their contract. The poor man's alcoholism and the needs of his family would be of no concern in the enforcement of the contract. However, in colonial America such a contract would most likely not have been enforced because of overriding concerns with community welfare. Equity, not contract law, would have prevailed. In a colonial parish, in which fair prices were set by community standards rather than by market conditions, and in which profiting from a neighbor's misfortune was regarded as sinful, the wealthy members of society assumed a duty to care for the poor and moral imperatives discouraged excessive drinking and encouraged the proper care of children.

One's position in the social hierarchy imposed duties that were reinforced by laws written to serve the public good, rather than to protect individual rights. Conversely, contract law derived from the basic Enlightenment truths of human equality and economic freedom. It recognized no privilege, but also no duty, beyond that expressed in the contract. It preserved the free wills of individual actors to pursue their own interests unencumbered by the values or restrictions of the government, the clergy, or social elite.[1] It recognized instead a moral relativism rooted in each person's ability to make his own decisions as to right, wrong, and relative moral values, so long as no criminal law was transgressed in the process.

Ironically, perhaps, the very belief system that asserts the existence of rights as absolutes that require free commerce and free government also recognizes moral judgment as a matter of individual conscience, and therefore a realm beyond group enforcement. Western political and economic structures, born in the Enlightenment, embrace a moral relativism.

Absolutist thought promotes a specific style of leadership. Truth creates parameters on the authority of leaders. An absolutist deduces action from truth: given that all men are equal and possessed of natural rights, how must governments function? Given that the law of supply and demand governs all economic exchanges, what must be the policy on wage controls? Morality is a private concern derived from individual belief. The respect of individual rights, including the right of conscience, precludes any assertion by one party as to what another equal party *should* do. In the age-old contest between protecting individual freedoms and serving the social good, the Enlightenment modernist likely favors the protection of individual freedoms, thereby avoiding prescriptions of duties, obligations, and roles.[2]

Natan Sharansky, chairman of the Adelson Institute for Strategic Studies in Israel, lends support for this proposition in his essay,

"Democracies Can't Compromise on Core Values." He notes the difference between the individualistic democracy of the United States and the communitarian democracies of Europe. In America, unlike in Europe, he writes, Muslim women "wear the veil in public schools or state colleges largely without controversy." In the United States, "the right to express one's identity is seen as fundamental." Americans' embrace of rights compels us to accept even that which is foreign to us or even threatens us. We have a long history of cultural relativism that can help us in going global today.[3]

This Enlightenment perspective has served as the foundation of Western laws and business practices for 200 years. Today's global leaders need a framework for working within cultures that have values different from those in the West. Though Enlightenment ideology is entirely Western, the moral relativism it espouses can serve as a Westerner's basis for cultural adaptation. To be successful in a global environment, business leaders must consider various factors that are key reflectors of cultural difference and embrace the people who hold different values even as they personally adhere to their own values. Respect and adaptation is essential; subordination or self-denial is not.

Framework for Cultural Values

Values are distinct from norms, although the two words are often mistakenly interchanged. *Norms* are societal rules. We are taught certain norms, such as respecting authority figures, at an early age because our cultural environment imposes them on us. Political correctness expresses a prevailing system of norms recognized in the late-twentieth and early-twenty-first centuries. Norms that become so well accepted as to provoke public censure in their breach can even become laws.

Values, on the other hand, are personal preferences. They often express what one hopes for in the society in which one finds oneself. Values can be absolute or relative. An ethic governing one in her behaviors with other people may be absolute. On the other hand, a person may value free time, but be willing to work 70 hours a week to advance in her career. The value assigned to free time is relative. Do you as an individual prefer the potential for security, achievement, recognition, or even money when choosing a career path? Most American leaders whom I coach don't rank money as the most important consideration. Generally, people find greater interest in those values they perceive as absolute. Such values may well be related more to what is good and what is bad, what is virtuous or what is evil. Individuals are drawn to groups of people that share common values. Members of a kibbutz share similar values in the same way that members of a street gang do. We also have the power to change our values. We challenge them as we mature and meet new people, read books, and form opinions. An intelligent mind will constantly be testing values. Individual values may not be consistent with society's norms. For example, I like to drive my car fast to get to my destination quickly (my value). But in my town, where on most streets the speed limit is unenforced, but the streets are marked to prevent passing, other drivers in front of me prevent me from speeding (our norm). People in any community must temper their desires to act on their own values by respect for prevailing norms. Business leaders working in foreign cultures must recognize both the prevailing norms of the foreign society and the values of the individuals with whom they work.

Success occurs when global leaders believe that other societies or cultures may have formed different values and norms from those to which they were accustomed—and then bridge those differences. For over 50 years, anthropologists have studied modern values and motivations. From Florence Kluckhoen and her associates at Harvard in the 1950s to scholars like Edward and Mildred Hall in the 1970s and continuing with Meena Wilson and Maxine Dalton at the Center for Creative Leadership in the late 1990s, scholars and practitioners laid the groundwork for the understanding of values by contemporary experts, such as Gary P. Ferraro. As Ferraro writes in his book *The Cultural Dimensions of International Business:* "If communication between people from different cultures is to be successful, each party must understand the cultural assumptions—or cultural starting points—of the other. Unfortunately, our own values, the result of cultural conditioning, are so much a part of our consciousness that we frequently fail to acknowledge their existence and consequently fail to understand that they may not be shared by people from other cultures. When that occurs, cross-cultural cues can be missed, communication becomes short-circuited, and hostilities can be generated."[4]

To help us better understand how different cultures encourage different values, Ferraro created a framework comprised of five dimensions that we can use to dissect the major themes that a culture's values might fall under. And to begin filling in these dimensions, Ferraro provides us with five questions, the answers to which will help us define the kinds of values embraced by particular cultures:

1. Do people identify themselves primarily as individuals or as members of a larger collective?
2. Do people with different levels of power and prestige treat one another equally or unequally?
3. To what extent do different cultures emphasize combat (tough) or compromise (tender)?
4. How do cultures differ in terms of taking risks, tolerating ambiguity, and needing relatively little organizational structure?
5. How precisely do people from different cultures deal with time?

Let's dig deeper into the implications that the answers to each of these questions convey.

Individual versus Collective Dimension

Many Western cultures, like those in the United States and the United Kingdom, tend to celebrate the strength of the individual and individual achievement. In such cultures, family ties tend to be subservient to those of the individual and self-sufficiency is an honored trait. Nations like Japan or Kenya, however, embrace a collective or group-oriented value orientation, in which people tend to identify or define themselves as members of a group rather than as individuals. As we discussed in Chapter 4, people in collectivist societies tend to think of the welfare of their families far more than in individualistic cultures like the United States. For example, an American company operating in Japan with Japanese employees must be sensitive to the notion that those workers think less about individual achievement than about how their efforts reflect on the group's achievement as a whole. Also, unlike the American ideal of self-sufficiency, Japanese workers highly value the interdependence that comes from working within a group. For leaders, that means creating incentives and recognizing achievements for groups rather than individuals. In this culture, a business should adopt a "high context," defined as keeping the volatility and variability of a group to a minimum. In many Asian cultures, awareness of the concept of "saving face" should restructure a Westerner's behavior. How another person is perceived within his or her group is important. Accordingly, you must never criticize an Asian individual in his own culture in public. Even praise should be done in a manner that does not isolate the individual from his group.

Crack in the Wall

The social contract of Japan, which has a historic and strong collective value system, is starting to change as a result of the depressed economic situation in the 1990s, sometimes referred to as the "lost decade," with declining job security and falling wages. Economic forces and a new global conscience of acceptable behavior may be partly responsible for this shift in values and the resultant determination of some employees to take the individual risk and pay the price of being a whistle-blower. The crack in the wall of silence from when business management encouraged fraudulent behavior and cover-ups is remarkable. A decade ago, reporting wrong-doing to the public never would have happened because the Japanese company was key to the employees' identity and position in society. There are still high personal costs when an employee blows the whistle on illegal behavior. The first major whistle-blower case in 2000 exposed the cover-up of accident-causing defects from products produced by Mitsubishi Motors, resulting in the arrest of executives and severe financial decline at this major formerly respected company. More and more whistle-blowers are coming forward, including Yoichi Mizutani who exposed fraud in the meat industry. Mitzutani explained, "I thought of how many small company owners in this industry, like me, lie awake at night, tormented by guilt over what they are doing. The industry talks of itself as one big family, which protects its own. But injustice is injustice."[5] After Mitzutani went public, he paid the price: He was driven out of business and his wife divorced him. However, his courage is now credited with opening the door for others to expose scandals, many of whom ask him for advice.

Equality versus Hierarchy Dimension

Whereas cultures like those found in the United States, Canada, or Sweden tend to share a value that people with different levels of power, prestige, and status can interact with each other as equals, the cultures of nations like Malaysia, Panama, and the Philippines respect social hierarchies based on a person's social status. This leads to higher status differences, formal social relations, and greater power concentrations among fewer people. This also means people who reside in lower rungs of the social order may have fewer perceived choices and rarely question authority. As a global leader coming from an egalitarian culture that might reward individuals that speak out or question authority figures, you may need to adjust your leadership approach if you want to create trust. It is crucial for you to define your rank and status at the onset of any relationship so that other individuals will know how to interact with you. You will also be expected to make the decisions affecting your organization with less input from subordinates, who will require active supervision.

Tough versus Tender Dimension

This dimension helps define a culture's attitude toward success. As Ferraro writes: "Do people in a particular society define success in terms of high-status, material accumulation, and well-rewarded jobs? Or do they define success in terms of less tangible rewards, such as quality time with friends and family, good working relationships, or opportunities for spiritual or personal growth?"[6] In other words, a "tough" culture has different preferences for achievement, assertiveness, power, competition, and material possessions, often at the expense of social relationships and cooperation. Tough societies also tend to enforce gender stereotypes, making it more difficult for women to join the workforce or to rise to positions of power. When working within a "tender" culture, on the other hand, leaders need to be sensitive to gender issues. Men may also assume more domestic roles and take an active role in raising the family. Tender cultures also reject the "winner take all" approach championed in tougher cultures. Leaders need to adjust how they conduct their outreach to members of each kind of culture. While individuals from tough cultures will respond to personal challenges, members of tender cultures will respond more positively to efforts that result in win-win scenarios for everyone involved.

Russia is a nation with a tough culture. BP, the global energy group operating in more than 100 countries, knew that its 50 percent investment in Russian oil company Tyumen Oil Co. (TNK) to create TNK-BP Ltd. in 2003 would be difficult, but also felt it had few choices if it wanted a major presence in and export ability from Russia. The CEO, Lord John Browne, knew the risks and commented at the time, "There is a toughness built into the culture of Russia. You have to cooperate."[7] In mid-2008, the Russian shareholders attempted a coup to remove the joint venture's CEO, Robert Dudley, formerly from Illinois and a long-term employee of Amoco, which was purchased by BP in 1998. He fled to an undisclosed location outside Russia, where he continued to operate as CEO after the Russian immigration service withdrew his visa and permission to work in the country. On August 14, 2008, the BP side suffered another setback with its troubled Russian joint venture after a Moscow court disqualified the venture's chief executive officer from holding corporate office in Russia for two years, according to the *New York Times*.[8] The issue was unresolved as this book was going to press, but one of the three Russian billionaires and a joint venture founding partner, Mikhail Fridman, indicated that the Russians were not going to leave, so ultimately some agreement would occur.

Dynamic versus Stable Dimension

This dimension refers to a culture's ability to tolerate ambiguity in its values and norms as opposed to formally enforcing those rules within a rigid structure. A key component of a dynamic culture is the ability of its members to tolerate uncertainty in the future and adapt to the unexpected. Cultures that are more comfortable with change have a greater tolerance for risk and have less emotional attachments to the status quo. At the same time, members of these cultures tend to be mobile, both in terms of geography and for whom they work. That creates challenges for organizations both to attract and to retain employees whom they have committed to training or promoting. From time to time, organizations may also have to rein in their employees who may be too eager to take risks and make decisions on the fly.

Organizations attempting to make inroads into more stable cultures, on the other hand, face a different challenge: specifically, how to encourage its members to embrace change, independent decision making and the taking of risks. Individuals who come from stable cultures tend to follow the letter of the law and rarely deviate from following rules or orders from a superior. These individuals also fear failure and thus will often play it safe—even when a situation clearly calls for a bit of bold decision making.

Time: Past, Present, or Future Dimension

Cultures express their differences in the way they think about time. Consider whether members from a culture have a precise interpretation of time—such as an appreciation for punctuality—or whether members have a more loose and fluid view of the time line for actions to be taken. American Indians, for example, begin all of their histories with the phrase, *in the past*. How long ago in the past is not important. Obviously, the challenge for leaders in organizations bridging from a punctual to a flexible culture is the ability to be patient. Another way to think about time's role in a culture is whether its members tend to focus on the past, the present, or the future. Past-oriented societies tend to regard prior experiences and events in the form of traditional wisdom as their guide to decision making. Present-focused cultures tend to think spontaneously and make decisions that maximize the impact of the moment, since they have little concern for what has happened before or what will come next. Future-focused societies will make sacrifices or investments today with the sole goal of reaping the benefits of those decisions down the road.

In Summary

Global leaders can use these five dimensions first to analyze where the subject culture rests on each of five spectra. If you think of each dimension as a spectrum or continuum (e.g., weighted toward the collective interest at one end or toward individuals' interests at the other), asking the questions that help define the dimension will reveal cultural clues that will help you to make decisions and act. These dimensions are helpful in connecting with a foreign culture by developing an understanding of the social norms. They can also be used to appreciate the values of particular organizations within the culture and where each falls on the spectrum compared to the societal norm. Just as the World Economic Forum competitive analysis by country ranks the pillars of competitiveness, you can use this five-dimension framework to determine cultures most similar to or different from your own. Since your habits were formed in your home country, being aware of different values and attitudes will serve you well in forming new habits.

The Dawn of Détente

In a parallel with some of the arguments fought in today's contemporary political campaigns, Richard Nixon, when he was serving in the Senate before he became the U.S. president was criticized for his public admission that he would be willing to meet and discuss the state of world affairs with his communist counterparts. Nixon, though, used the controversy as an opportunity to hold a public debate with Soviet premier Nikita Khrushchev on July 24, 1959—an event he used to promote the difference in values between Washington, DC, and Moscow. Yet, within a shared context of competition, he named consumerism as a more effective method for spreading the notion of democracy than the building of more bombs. The following was taken from a transcript printed in the *New York Times* the following day:[9]

> NIXON: We do not claim to astonish the Russian people. We hope to show our diversity and our right to choose. We do not wish to have decisions made at the top by government officials who say that all homes should be built in the same way. Would it not be better to compete in the relative merits of washing machines than in the strength of rockets? Is this the kind of competition you want?
>
> KHRUSHCHEV: Yes that's the kind of competition we want. But your generals say: Let's compete in rockets. We are strong and we can beat you. But in this respect we can also show you something.
>
> NIXON: To me you are strong and we are strong. In some ways, you are stronger. In others, we are stronger. We are both strong not only from the standpoint of weapons but also from the standpoint of will and spirit. Neither should use that strength to put the other in a position where he in effect has an ultimatum. In this day and age that misses the point. With modern weapons it does not make any difference if war comes. We both have had it.

In other words, competition in the marketplace, rather than on battlefields, can be the proving ground of different value systems. Consumers and employees are drawn to the value propositions from great companies like Johnson & Johnson and the Tata Group as a result of their clear and relevant consumer and employer brands.

Societal Values and Employer Brands

Each year, *Fortune* magazine, in partnership with the Great Place to Work Institute, compiles a list of the 100 Best Companies to Work For in America. Companies like American Express, Cisco Systems, Amgen, Starbucks, and Intel are some of the names that regularly appear on the list. When you look for what all these companies have in common, you find that each of them has implemented employee relations programs expressive of certain values held by that corporation, such as offering ample training opportunities, more effective and more important to employees than those programs implemented by their industry peers. Given the fact that employees will seek out employers that share similar values, the importance of promoting a company's social values—a practice that has come to be known as *employer branding*—is becoming increasingly significant. As Mark Hornung, senior vice president at Bernard Hodes Group, a leading recruitment company, writes:

> *Employees have become cynical about employment because of the layoffs that occurred during the recent recession. They no longer see any reward in being loyal to their employer; rather, they look for what the employer can offer them in terms of career development or skills enhancement—both of which make the employee more marketable on the labor scene. More fundamentally, the baby boomers, Gen X and the Millennials [sic Gen Y] are the first generations to grow up with the mass media. These generations are a very brand-oriented cohort of consumers. They make their decisions based on brands—in other words, the relationship the potential employee or consumer has with an organization. If the brand is unknown or negatively perceived, it will be much more difficult for that company to attract employees or customers.[10]*

When it comes to attracting and retaining talent in the inter-connected economy, where everyone is chasing the same pools of talent, employers need to start adopting the marketing techniques they have traditionally used for consumers and turn them into tools for attracting and keeping employees. Just as in consumer market-ing, where brands have strong values attached to them that reflect a product's quality and reputation, employer brands can convey what a company thinks about its employees in terms of loyalty, training, and career advancement opportunities. Companies like Procter & Gamble, UPS, and Microsoft have developed employer brands to convey their values and connect with employees, particularly Gen Y employees with their sense of entitlement when looking for their next career move. It is important to note that exploiting the power of employer brands is not just an issue for leaders based in the devel-oped world. As more and more multinationals move into emerging markets, and new opportunities arise around the world, emerging market multinationals find their talent pools under attack.

As we discussed in Chapter 1, as well as in Chapter 5, business leaders will increasingly find themselves feeling the pinch of the laws of supply and demand when it comes to the realities of the new global labor force. We know, for example, that due to the aging pop-ulations in the developed countries, the face of tomorrow's work-force will come from emerging markets and the competition has already begun as multinationals from both developed and emerg-ing markets have moved aggressively to tap these new pipelines. But even these new talent pools won't be sufficient to keep up with demand—particularly for highly skilled workers proficient in future growth sectors like computers, engineering, and biochemicals. That means that organizations not only face the challenge of meeting the spiraling costs of recruiting highly-skilled talent from around the world, they also have to shift their organization's internal incentives in order to retain their best workers.

I recently had the opportunity to discuss this challenge facing today's global leaders with Peter Cheese, managing partner for tal-ent and organizational performance at Accenture. Cheese co-wrote a book (with Robert J. Thomas and Elizabeth Craig) that tackles this subject, called *The Talent Powered Organization: Strategies for Globalization, Talent Management and High Performance.*[11] In both his client work at Accenture and his book, Cheese addresses what he sees as the key problem facing global businesses over the next decade: companies need to use targeted marketing and word-of-mouth goodwill to attract talent. As demographic shifts are helping to shake the globe in terms of making it increasingly difficult for companies to attract and retain the talent they need, companies are not focusing adequately on how they can take leading positions in the talent game by promoting their corporate values through their employer brand. "And the first step in doing so," he added, "is to understand how that employer brand is already perceived in the talent market."[12]

One example of a company making headway in developing an employer brand is Larsen & Toubro (L&T), one of India's largest construction companies. Cheese recounted part of his conversation with L&T's CEO and division heads regarding the recruiting problems the company faced. India has long had a large pool of semi-skilled workers for L&T to engage in its various construction projects, the executive told him, but more and more of these workers emigrated to countries undergoing huge construction booms, like Dubai, where they can earn (tax-free) three-times the salary that can be earned in India. That meant L&T, founded in 1938, needed to learn about how to access new talent pools—or create them. While L&T has begun recruiting immigrant workers of its own from China as well as developing training programs to groom new domestic workers, the company lost four out of every five employees it trained to competitors in other markets. The key recognition for the CEO was not only to begin training more domestic workers in a joint partnership with local and national government support, but also for L&T "to build an employer brand to try and attract the kinds of skilled people they had taken for granted."[13]

A major challenge for some organizational leaders in building brands for their company is overcoming perceptions associated with its industry. Companies like L&T or BASF, the German chemical giant, for instance, face the challenge of making the skills and daily job responsibilities required for construction or chemical manufacturing attractive to a generation that values environmental and social responsibility. In the past, chemical engineers did not have many choices of a career, but now they can use their academic training to join software and information technology firms that ostensibly are more innovative. L&T focuses on the positive aspects of working in the construction business, such as its role in modernizing a country's aging infrastructure. BASF focuses on the innovation from new chemicals creating breakthroughs in everything from new medicines to environmentally-friendly substitutes, replacing oil-based products. The goal is to reposition the brand to be more attractive to its target audience—namely potential recruits.

"What companies cannot do is build false promises into their brands by claiming to be something they aren't," Cheese explained. If a company fails to deliver on its brand promise, it will not only disenfranchise current employees, it will turn away potential ones. Word-of-mouth marketing can work against the power of the brand just as well as it can help it. With new social networking job-hunting sites like www.Vault.com, all it can take is for one unhappy recruit or employee to post a disparaging comment about a company to turn off legions of others. "You know that old saying where [sic] if someone likes a product, he will tell ten people, but if he hates it, he will tell 100," Cheese continued. "With the power of the Internet, you can multiply that by an order of magnitude." This is why securing a position as one of the 100 Best Companies to Work For is valuable. Receiving an award from an objective arbiter can convey a sense of pride to your current employees and transmit an attractive message to potential recruits.

For example, Tesco, the U.K.-based supermarket giant, was facing tough times back in 1993 when, faced with new competition from discount chains, its share price slipped 40 percent. But after the company evaluated its position, it decided to refocus on promoting its core values, or "employee brand position" that included things like trust, respect, and teamwork along with training and pay increases for its staff of 12,000 managers. Tesco established an annual review process by which the company surveys its staff as to how true the company has been to its core values. Not only did those investments in the company brand provide returns in a turnaround of the firm's share price, it also attracted accolades from observers like *HR Magazine*, which named Tesco the United Kingdom's top company for recruiting and retaining talent, and *Management Today*, which named it the United Kingdom's most admired company. "We've had to change completely the way we manage," said Terry Leahy, Tesco's CEO. "What is important is to live the values. They have to be central to the way you manage in order to affect processes and projects and how people work. It's been evolution, not revolution. Rapid evolution."[14]

As the Tesco example shows, focusing on the values that comprise an employer brand is not merely a "nice to have"; it is a critical asset for any company looking to compete in the interconnected economy. When building such a brand, leaders need to focus on the five dimensions that make up the framework of values—Individual and Collective, Equality and Hierarchy, Tough and Tender, Dynamic and Stable, and the three perspectives on Time—in order to understand how the values associated with their employer brand will translate into the local culture from which they are recruiting and employing workers. This exercise, which objectively matches up an organization's values with those of a specific culture, can help leaders in understanding whether their organization might, in fact, fit well into that society's fabric. While it might be possible to shift an organization's values, cultural values rarely change—which means organizations need to do their homework in understanding where they might achieve their best results and not just assume that every culture will enable those results.

Johnson & Johnson: A Company Driven by Ethics

Johnson & Johnson, the pharmaceutical, medical devices and consumer packaged goods manufacturer, is one example of the breed of global companies that attract talent based on the strength of its employer brand. Specifically, the core of the company's values is its deep commitment to ethics—a message that it communicates to its field offices around the world in 36 languages. Even though the company credo is more than 50 years old, its message—printed and hung on the wall at every company location—rings crisply even today. The order of priorities in this credo reflects the order of importance of each constituency: doctors, nurses, patients, parents, employees, communities, and stockholders.

The Johnson & Johnson Credo[15]

We believe our first responsibility is to the doctors, nurses and patients, to mothers and fathers and all others who use our products and services. In meeting their needs everything we do must be of high quality. We must constantly strive to reduce our costs in order to maintain reasonable prices. Customers' orders must be serviced promptly and accurately. Our suppliers and distributors must have an opportunity to make a fair profit.

We are responsible to our employees, the men and women who work with us throughout the world. Everyone must be considered as an individual. We must respect their dignity and recognize their merit. They must have a sense of security in their jobs. Compensation must be fair and adequate, and working conditions clean, orderly and safe. We must be mindful of ways to help our employees fulfill their family responsibilities.

Employees must feel free to make suggestions and complaints. There must be equal opportunity for employment, development and advancement for those qualified. We must provide competent management, and their actions must be just and ethical.

We are responsible to the communities in which we live and work and to the world community as well. We must be good citizens—support good works and charities and bear our fair share of taxes. We must encourage civic improvements and better health and education. We must maintain in good order the property we are privileged to use, protecting the environment and natural resources.

Our final responsibility is to our stockholders. Business must make a sound profit. We must experiment with new ideas. Research must be carried on, innovative programs developed and

*mistakes paid for. New equipment must be purchased, new fa-
cilities provided and new products launched. Reserves must be
created to provide for adverse times. When we operate according
to these principles, the stockholders should realize a fair return.*

Context of Values for Courageous Leadership

As Henry B. Veatch explains in his book, *Rational Man: A Modern
Interpretation of Aristotelian Ethics*, the only way a social organization
can function properly is if there are shared absolute truths—trouble
arises if these truths are somehow open to interpretation. As Veatch
writes: "It is true that as the conditions of life vary from age to age,
from region to region, from one culture to another, the criteria of
bravery, say, or of honesty, or of stupidity will vary considerably.
But the distinction between bravery and cowardice, honesty and
dishonesty, wisdom and folly, will nonetheless be recognized and
maintained almost universally."[16]

To make the best decisions in our lives and careers, we must use
a combination of these universal virtues such as honesty, integrity,
discipline, and courage. When it comes to going global, the virtue
that is most often tested is courage—namely the courage to overcome the fear that accompanies change and taking prudent risks.
Some leaders may be defensive and think the level of courage and
risk taking that worked well in the past will continue to work well.
Not so. With the acceleration of change, new competitors, and difficulty to find and keep the talent needed to get the job done, a new
level of courage to push beyond traditional methods is required to
be a leader going global with his or her business. That's why, when
we test leaders for their CQ scores, we ask them to evaluate the
organization's values exemplified in their experience and the employer brand. Assessments help us reach critical insights about each
individual because his or her personal value system needs to align
with the organization's norms that embrace or at the least, support

similar values. We use the following 10 categories to determine leader preference profiles:

1. *Structure:* What kind of chain of command exists in your workplace? Do you prefer to have a clear chain to follow or do you thrive in a more flexible chain such as a management matrix? Some leaders thrive only where they know exactly to whom they report and who reports to them. On the other hand, many individuals prefer situations like those that are prevalent in the movie industry, where you might find yourself reporting to a new director each film, changing every several months when the production ends.

2. *Decision making:* Does your ideal organization make decisions through directive, participative, or consensus means?

3. *Speed of decisions:* What about the speed by which those decisions are made—do you prefer environments where decisions happen at a slow, medium, or fast pace? What type of an industry matches this speed of decision making?

4. *Profit planning approach:* Are profits planned by a top-down or bottom-up approach? Or, is there a negotiation between the two? Since nonprofit organizations have different metrics from a publicly traded organization, we would assess how goals such as fund-raising are measured by the board, the executive director, or in collaboration with both.

5. *Communication style:* Does your organization employ a careful and formal approach to communicating? At the other end of the spectrum, does your boss use a direct style, perhaps open and informal?

6. *Conflict style:* Many organizations run into problems when they impute their values without putting them into a global context. How does your organization go about solving conflict—by avoiding it, by accommodating it, by simply asserting it, or by actively resolving it?

7. *Intellectual emphasis:* Does your organization embrace an analytical, a creative, or an intuitive approach to thinking through new ideas and innovation?

8. *Ethical approach:* When it comes to ethics in the workplace, do you feel most comfortable in an organization that takes a situational approach to ethics (exemplified by the folks at Enron), a legalistic approach (where following the letter of the law is the norm in the workplace), or a values-driven approach to ethics, such as that used by companies like Johnson & Johnson. (See sidebar for more on Johnson & Johnson's value-driven approach.)

9. *Pace of product development:* When it comes to introducing new products or services into the market, do you prefer organizations that employ a time frame that is long (such as pharmaceutical companies that can take years to develop new drugs suitable for the market), medium (product cycles measured in years or months), or short (such as consumer products companies where some product cycles are measured in months or weeks)?

10. *Life cycle of business:* When it comes to finding your role as a leader, do you prefer to join an organization that is mature, moderate, high growth, turn around, or in its startup stage? Your choice can depend on your appetite for hierarchy and risk-taking. Again, the choice comes back to linking your values with the context of the decision.

Preferences in these 10 categories can greatly help you chart an organization's norms reflective of its values as compared to your personal values. It is one thing for a leader to feel courageous, but when that leader knows the organization shares and understands a multicultural value system—he will have a strong platform to stand on when making the decisions that will shape the future course of that organization. Finding an organization in which diverse cultures are welcomed and understood can lead to a positive and engaging experience for the employee. You may think, "Now I understand what has been missing," or "This is why I love working in my organization so much." Understanding preferences using the framework described will give leaders the tools to align organizations with common values and shape the future of the interconnected economy.

Remaining True to Yourself

Before you can adapt to values, you must first understand your own values and motivations. Companies seek to portray *their* employer brand through a clear definition of the skills and capabilities required for the job, discovering talent and then developing and deploying the talent effectively. *You* must create your own value proposition. One way to begin is to define the skills you want to develop and what motivates you.

In their book, *Just Enough: Tools for Creating Success in Your Work and Life*, Laura Nash and Howard Stevenson from the Harvard Business School, explore the notion that Americans, in particular, are cursed with the notion to "best the best" even though when we rank achievement above all standards, we often fall victim to our excesses.[17] Quite correctly the authors ask, as we continue to strive for loftier and loftier goals, will we lose the ability to recognize what is "just enough" to realize a degree of satisfaction in what we have already accomplished? In putting this point in perspective, the authors rely on philosophical foundations, as they write: "The tragedian Sophocles, in his famous 'Ode on Man' in the play *Antigone*, marveled at humankind's resourcefulness and success: The chorus notes that without gills, man has devised ways to travel on the sea. He has invented speech, and plows for the Earth. With these accomplishments he secures good things such as food, shelter, the rule of cities, and complicated forms of reasoning. But, argues the wise chorus, 'from death alone he still cannot escape. . . .' Limitation is built in to the human condition. You need to bend to higher laws."

To be a leader in the interconnected world means that you need to be true to yourself and your personal values. Once you understand how to keep your ambitions in context and consistent with your personal preferences, you'll be free to overcome your fears and successfully embrace globalization and all the messy details that might accompany it.

Key Points to Consider

- Step one in defining your own set of values is to begin by writing them down. Make note of areas where your personal values may be in conflict with societal norms.

- How do your personal values match up with the norms that exist in your current organization?

- What other organizations around the world do you think might share similar values to your own? How can you establish an alliance with such an organization?

- How can you improve the connection between your organization's brand and the values you want to emulate?

- What personal values will help you connect with other cultures and their values?

The Final Stop

Now that we have nearly completed our journey, it is time to prepare for our final stop: a way-station of sorts where we can both stop to catch our breath and spend some thinking about the tools you will need to continue this journey around the globe on your own. Business around the globe is moving fast. The globe is shaking even as you read this. It is time to transform your own thinking to take advantage of the new opportunities that lie before you.

Epilogue: Continuing Your Journey to New Horizons

When I started writing this book, I thought about the important questions that Peter Drucker would ask a CEO to help him frame his thinking and strategy for action. He would ask five essential questions: What is our mission? Who is our customer? What does the customer value? What are our results? What is our plan? I asked myself those questions when thinking about international business opportunities and risks and how I would help individuals embrace the hard work, sometimes fun and always life-changing experiences of expanding his or her business experience to new areas outside his or her home country. It struck me that when the globe is shaking in the world of business, some lucky folks will understand and react to the fast-paced interconnected business dynamics we face. They are the best of the best.

Others might read this book and the headlines thinking, "That's good for other folks, but I will just worry about my corner of the world." I consider the latter's attitudes as reflective of the good trying to stay good, but failing. If you do not adapt, you cannot stay good.

Still others might say, "Put up walls, protect what we have, prevent the globe from shaking as long as we can." Unfortunately, an ostrich with his head in the sand will quickly lose his breath and expire. No one can prevent the dynamics of today's business world. But, you can shape events.

Shaking the globe and finding a way to succeed will require an athlete's mentality. The reason sport is an apt metaphor is that both business and athletics require individuals who excel in their field with competence and use quantitative tools to measure progress in developing mental toughness. Going global requires the mental capacity to synthesize what is happening and the physical ability to travel and to handle tough situations wherever and whenever they occur. Not everyone will succeed at being a global citizen, but many can make a contribution to the success of their organizations that do so. In the process, they adapt and survive. At the very least, they read the daily news with a perspective from this book about the increasingly democratic and interdependent world to overcome the fear that public figures like Lou Dobbs foment by playing on the economic uncertainty from the changing world.

Four years ago, I watched an episode of *Lou Dobbs Tonight* as I sat and waited in a hotel room to meet a colleague for dinner. Dobbs was ranting about the horrors of outsourcing and the trouble with American business. At first, I thought this was an isolated case of trying to improve TV ratings, but my research convinced me that he flipped from being a champion of capitalism to an opportunist who could draw more attention to himself if he played the role of a demagogue. It's not just conservative pundits who find his logic flawed. *Mother Jones* published an article about how Lou Dobbs changed when Fox News muscled its way into cable and "its ability to harness the collective anger of large swaths of the country that felt ignored. . . . Perhaps more than his peers, Dobbs has used cable's niche messaging and agitated viewers to refigure the role of news anchor."[1]

Remarkably, CNN President Jon Klein unabashedly states the goal of his network is to reassert their primacy in political news coverage and admires how Lou Dobbs' antics "shows you something about the power media can have away from the centers of power [sic, like New York]. That's one of Lou's strengths. He speaks to the people and he also speaks to the influencers."[2] I tolerate his entertainment value, but worry that his charming affable persona masks the real story about staying competitive and being a courageous leader in business today.

I hope you will come away with three key messages from this book. First, we need to understand how the world is interconnected and that all the people in it are interdependent as we share natural resources, human resources, and capital funds. We need to transcend our nationality. We don't abandon our national pride, but at the same time, we don't have a "center-of-the-universe-is-where-I-am" perspective. To understand cross-cultural perspectives, we need to observe actions and decision-making processes in different parts of the globe with mindfulness and empathy. The pace of change is faster than in the past as a result of technology, communications, education, and more porous borders than we have ever experienced in the history of mankind. If we don't participate, we will be left behind. Just as the athlete who decides to take a year off from practice may never recover his competitive advantage, time is of the essence in keeping in touch and operating in the multi-polar world.

Second, we must face the financial realities that created this need for going global. Even something as staid and predictable as accounting for financial results seems to be shaken to its very roots. Using IFRS and communicating financial figures with new assumptions and under new guidelines will shake the globe for a few years. Once this new reporting requirement becomes generally understood, the transparency and comparability of financial results and return on investment will help people make better resource-allocation decisions and smarter investments for the future. But if accounting can change so radically, we have to wonder if there is any refuge in which to hide from the competition and changes required in today's world.

Given the options, it's better to lead change with courage rather than continue in an anachronistic, conventional, or compliant manner. Challenging old assumptions is the first step to being a courageous leader, but individuals cannot do this alone. Each of us needs to find a way to integrate into the business system to enroll followers. Use innovation to transform an organization or even start a new business to be more competitive. The five points to consider at the end of each chapter were designed to provoke self-reflection to encourage acts of courage. The key message is to combine your competency, curiosity, caring, and perseverance to be a courageous leader in the twenty-first century.

Third, we should become aware of the six forces shaping personal courage if we are to go global. Namely, we experience different cultural norms as evident through beliefs, family, and time horizons; communicate with youth in new ways; tap into the talents of women; understand shareholder interests; capture the entrepreneurial drive for innovation; and respect individuals' value systems. Adapting to different cultural norms may, at first, make us uncomfortable. The unifying message is that lifelong learning never stops. It becomes more critical as we progress in our careers and our lives.

As you respond to this shaking globe, you can make a difference by doing several things differently in the weeks and months ahead. I offer some practical suggestions for you to consider as you create your own discipline to embrace this shaking globe, steady it, and move forward with confidence:

- *Seek help from other global citizens.* There are many programs available for practitioners, activists, journalists, and scholars. For example, the National Endowment for Democracy invites applicants to the Reagan-Fascell Democracy Fellows program open to citizens of all countries. This 10-month program was established to support democratic activists, human rights advocates, journalists, and others who work on the frontlines of democracy promotion in emerging and aspiring democracies.

- *Seek knowledge.* The Peterson Institute for International Economics is an example of one of many private, nonprofit, nonpartisan research institutions. It is devoted to the study of international economic policy. Since 1981, the Institute has provided timely and objective analysis of, and concrete solutions to, a wide range of international economic problems. It is one of the very few economics think tanks that are widely regarded as "nonpartisan" by the press and "neutral" by Congress, and the quality media cites it more than any other such institution.

- *Seek competence.* My hope is that after reading this book, you will be inspired to take your next step toward shaking the globe.

Acknowledgments

Writing this book has been a journey for me. It began after my first book, *Fit In, Stand Out* (New York: McGraw-Hill) was published in 2005. I thought I would never devote the time and energy to writing another book. However, I have come to know many extraordinary people through my speaking and in-house executive education programs that resulted from that book. I listened to their comments and questions. Each person wanted answers for specific dilemmas he or she was facing and wanted insight to manage the onslaught of change. Reflecting on the root cause of the changes, I discovered that many questions rose from cultural differences and a desire to know how to get along better with others to be effective at work and feel secure in understanding what might happen next. I also realized that many Americans feared the economic changes that are happening.

In the process of researching and writing, I discovered that you can learn something from almost any situation. I thank all of the people who shared personal stories and suggestions for *Shaking the Globe*. I am particularly grateful to the following people for their help: Dean Nancy Bagranoff, Kevin Cox, Cathy and Bruce Cranston, Darren Dahl, Philippe Dauman, Candace Duncan, Francis Flavin,

Jay Fishman, Eric Foss, Sue Green, Das Gucharan, Cathy Higgins, Dennis Hightower, Dr. Brian Jaski, Cathy Lewis, Laura Martin, Patricia McCulloch, Ed Merkle, Deb Morrin, Karim Sahyoun, Marta Stewart, Howard Stoeckel, Bob Thomas, Nick Thorne, Helene Uhlfelder, Meg Weston, and Stephen Yas I benefited greatly from these thoughtful individuals who provided feedback and ideas during the research process or read and commented on my manuscript.

Bill Green suggested that some of the multi-polar world research that Accenture folks did and presented at the World Economic Forum in Davos, Switzerland, might be useful and offered to connect me with the authors. Midway through my writing, after I read several years of research reports, I recognized the synchronicity of the Accenture data and my personal experience. I give thanks to Peter Cheese, Mark Foster, and Mark Spelman for their deep knowledge of global business, their dialogues, and their insights.

Dr. Altaf Merchant, assistant professor at the University of Washington, did an outstanding job of analyzing the research surveys of courageous (and not so courageous) leaders, helping shape the questions and proving the value derived from the Courage Quotient assessment tool. His own global experiences and academic study of nostalgia as a motivator reminded me of my many professors from Kellogg business school, from whom I still learn.

My husband, Mark, deserves special mention because he encourages me, edits my writing, and implores me to keep on point. He understands my need to travel, to study, and sometimes to be a little late to come to dinner. No one can understand how much his unwavering support and deepest affection inspires me to live my life to its fullest and attempt to make a difference in this world. His love of history and philosophy continues to enrich my life and inform my work. Thank you, Mark, for being you.

Finally, this book would not be in your bookstore if it were not for my agent Reid Boates, my publisher Matt Holt, and the team at John Wiley & Sons, including Christine Moore, Jessica Campilango, Kim Dayman, Christine Kim, and Peter Knapp. I am grateful for your enthusiasm, support, and hard work.

Notes

Part I: Preparing for an Adventure
Chapter 1: Today's Interconnected Globe

1. Philip Stephens, "A Global Response Is Needed to the Shifting World Order," *Financial Times*, November 30, 2007.

2. Accenture, Economist Intelligence Unit, "The Rise of the Multi-Polar World," 2007, 5.

3. Parag Khanna, "Waving Goodbye to Hegemony," *New York Times*, January 27, 2008.

4. Accenture, "The Rise of the Multi-Polar World," 2.

5. Eduardo Porter, "Europe Fears a Post-Bush Unilateralism, This Time on Trade," *New York Times*, June 7, 2008.

6. "Ten Trends to Watch in 2006," *McKinsey Quarterly*, January 17, 2006.

7. Chris Suellentrop, "The Isolationist," *New York Times Book Review*, January 27, 2008.

8. Background based on Dobbs' *CNN* news platform (www.cnn.com) as well as his book, *Exporting America: Why Corporate Greed is Shipping American Jobs Overseas* (New York: Warner Business Books, 2004).

9. Accenture, "The Rise of the Multi-Polar World," 1.

10. Ronald Reagan, June 12, 1987, www.reaganfoundation.org/reagan/speeches/wall.asp.

11. Eurostat statistics, http://epp.eurostat.ec.europa.eu.

12. Parag Khanna, "Waving Goodbye to Hegemony," *New York Times Magazine*, January 27, 2008.

13. Andrew Bounds, "Globalisation Enriches EU, Study Says," *Financial Times*, February 29, 2008.

14. "New Rules for a Globalized World," *Aspen Idea*, Summer 2005.

15. The World Economic Forum, *The Global Competitiveness Report 2007–2008*, www.weforum.org.

16. "More Visas, More Jobs," *Wall Street Journal*, March 19, 2008.

17. Martin Fackler, "Michelin Gives Stars, but Tokyo Turns Up Nose," *New York Times*, February 24, 2008.

18. Michael Schwirtz, "A New Miracle on Ice: Russia Is Luring Back N.H.L. Stars," *New York Times*, February 29, 2008.

19. Khanna, "Waving Goodbye to Hegemony."

20. Leila Heckman, "Refuge from Volatility Could Be Found via New Frontiers," *Financial Times*, February 14, 2008.

21. Joel Kurtzman and Glenn Yago, *Global Edge* (Watertown, MA: Harvard Business School Press, 2008).

22. Author interview with Mark Foster with research quoted from Accenture, "The Rise of the Multi-Polar World"; and Accenture, "The Rise of the Emerging-Market Multinational," 2008.

23. Peter Marsh, "Erie Monsters Are This Year's GE Favorite for Immelt," *Financial Times*, January 18, 2008.

24. Stephen Wisnefski, "Overseas Growth Lifts Caterpillar," *Wall Street Journal*, January 26–27, 2008.

25. Peter Drucker, *The Daily Drucker: 366 Days of Insight and Motivation for Getting the Right Things Done* (New York: HarperCollins, 2004), 42.

26. Justin Martin, "The Global CEO," *Chief Executive*, January–February 2004.

Chapter 2: Financial Realities

1. "Chart Focus Newsletter," *McKinsey Quarterly*, January 2008; "The World in 2008," *Economist*, 2007; "The New Face of Hunger," *Economist*, April 19, 2008.

2. "Why Cheap Oil May Be Bad," *Economist*, March 4, 1999.

3. Jad Mouawad, "Oil Price Rise Fails to Open Tap," *New York Times*, April 29, 2008; see also Jad Mouawad, "The Big Thirst," *New York Times*, April 20, 2008.

4. "The New Face of Hunger," *Economist*, April 17, 2008.

5. "Corn Prices Will Remain in Record High Territory," *Wall Street Journal*, May 10–11, 2008.

6. Mark Bittman, "Rethinking the Meat-Guzzler," *New York Times*, January 27, 2008.

7. Veronika Oleksyn, Associated Press, "UN Secretary-General Calls Food Price Rise a Global Crisis," April 25, 2008; Associated Press, "Sam's Club: Costco Limit Bulk Rice Purchases," April 24, 2008.

8. Bittman, "Rethinking the Meat-Guzzler."

9. Jonathan Birchall, "Wal-Mart to Push 1,000 Chinese Suppliers to Adopt a Green Agenda," *Financial Times*, April 7, 2008.

10. James Surowiecki, "Iceland's Deep Freeze," *New Yorker*, April 21, 2008.

11. Ibid.

12. Holly Morris, "Searching for the Dalai Lama," *New York Times Book Review*, April 6, 2008.

13. Peter S. Goodman and Louise Story, "Overseas Investors Buy U.S. Holdings at a Record Pace," *New York Times*, January 20, 2008.

14. To read more about the causes see *Wikipedia*, s.v. "hyperinflation," http://en.wikipedia.org/wiki/Hyperinflation#Hyperinflation_around _the_world/.

15. Countries tracked include: Australia, France, Germany, Japan, Korea, Mexico, Spain, the United Kingdom, and the United States; see the Conference Board's latest research, www.conference-board.org/ economics/.

16. Conference Board, "2007 Annual Report," www.conference-board.org/pdf_free/AnnualReport2007.pdf.

17. Ben Stein, "Wall Street, Run Amok," *New York Times*, April 27, 2008.

18. Paul J. Lim, "A Storm May Lift the Heat," *New York Times*, April 13, 2008.

19. Thomas M. Humphrey, "Analyst of Change," *Region Focus*, Fall 2007; see also Joseph Schumpeter, *Capitalism, Socialism and Democracy*

(New York: Routledge, 2006); Thomas K. McCraw, *Prophet of Innovation: Joseph Schumpeter and Creative Destruction* (Cambridge, MA: Belknap Press, 2007).

20. Herb Greenberg, "A Columnist's Parting Advice," *Wall Street Journal*, April 26, 2008.

21. Sarah Johnson, "IFRS: No Longer If, but When," February 8, 2008, CFO.com; see also the International Accounting Standards Board web site, www.iasb.org, and a roundup of case studies on the nations who have successfully adopted IFRS on the web site for the United Nations Conference on Trade and Development, www.unctad.org.

22. Sarah Johnson, "The Revenue-Recognition Rules Paradox," February 5, 2008, CFO.com.

23. Marie Leone, "FASB's Herz Calls for 'Choice with a Timetable,'" November 12, 2007, CFO.com.

24. See also the Norfolk Southern Corp. web site, www.nscorp.com.

25. Author interview with Marta Stewart, May 8, 2008.

26. Accenture, "The Rise of the Emerging-Market Multinational," 2008.

27. Peter Drucker, *The Daily Drucker: 366 Days of Insight and Motivation for Getting the Right Things Done* (New York: HarperCollins, 2004), 42.

28. International Monetary Fund and Thomson Financial.

29. Goldman Sachs, "Global Economics Paper No: 141," May 1, 2006.

30. Accenture, "Multi-Polar World 2: The Rise of the Emerging-Market Multinational," 2007.

31. Ibid., 1.

32. Goldman Sachs, "Getting Globalization Right: Meeting the Challenge of the Century." For more information see "Global Economics Paper 95," July 23, 2005; and GS Global Economic web site, https://portal.gs.com (subscription required).

33. Author notes from a discussion with Charlene Barshefsky on the role of the United States in an increasingly global world, May 9, 2008.

Chapter 3: The Four Types of Leaders

1. *Webster's II New Riverside Dictionary*, rev. ed. (Boston: Houghton Mifflin, 1996).

2. Author interviews with the subject; see also *Notable Names Database*, s.v. "John H. Bryan," www.nndb.com/people/986/000060806/.

3. This tool is a proven resource, analyzed by a PhD through regression analysis, using results from men and women in many different organizations from all over the world.

4. To ascertain your CQ score, visit www.FISOfactor.com. You will take a 10- to 15-minute survey with results sent to you via e-mail by the end of the month. This offer is available for one month after the publication date of the book.

5. The survey was conducted from August 2007 to January 2008.

6. Michael Lewis, "The New Organization Man," October 30, 1997, Slate.com; see also William H. Whyte, *The Organization Man* (Philadelphia: University of Pennsylvania Press, 2002) and Sloan Wilson, *The Man in the Gray Flannel Suit* (New York: Four Walls Eight Windows, 2002).

7. Patrick McGeehan, "Meltdown Didn't Hurt His Golf Game," *New York Times*, July 8, 2007; Grant Gross, "Networking Execs Sentenced for Accounting Fraud," *Network World*, July 3, 2007.

8. Pui-Wing Tam, "H-P's Board Ousts Fiorina as CEO," *Wall Street Journal*, February 10, 2005; Pui-Wing Tam, "Hewlett-Packard Board Considers a Reorganization: Management Moves Stem from Performance Concerns—Helping Fiorina 'Succeed,'" *Wall Street Journal*, January 24, 2005; Peter Burrows and Ben Elgin, "The Surprise Player behind the Coup at HP," *BusinessWeek*, March 14, 2005; Paul R. La Monica, CNN/Money, "Fiorina Out, HP Stock Soars," February 10, 2005; see also Carly Fiorina, *Tough Choices: A Memoir* (Kirkwood, NY: Portfolio Hardcover, 2006).

9. Author correspondence with John H. Bryan; see also Robert Johnson, "From Sara Lee to Charities," *New York Times*, March 6, 2005; David Barboza, "Sara Lee Sets Timetable for Shift in Power," *New York Times*, January 28, 2000.

10. See Ms. Winfrey's biography, www2.oprah.com/about/press/about_press_pressroom.jhtml; see also George Mair, *Oprah Winfrey: The Real Story* (New York: Carol Publishing Group, 1995).

11. See Amar Bose's official biography, www.bose.com; see also a profile on MIT's web site, http://web.mit.edu/invent/iow/bose.html.

12. See www.myprimetime.com/work/ge/schultzbio/.

13. See http://video.msn.com/?mkt=en-us&fg=rss&vid=7a40317b -d3aa-440d-b827-ac82b2ba540b&from=imbot_default/ (accessed May 3, 2008).

14. As quoted in an interview by Ed Bradley with Mr. Woods on CBS news show *60 Minutes*, September 3, 2006 (transcript available, www. cbsnews.com/stories/2006/03/23/60minutes/main1433767 _page2.shtml); see also the official biographies of Mr. Woods at www .tigerwoods.com and one provided by the Professional Golfer's Tour, www.pgatour.com/ players/00/87/93/.

Part II: Connecting the World in Six Stops
Chapter 4: Cultural Norms

1. Robert W. Fogel, "Capitalism & Democracy in 2040," *Daedalus*, Summer 2007, 87–95.

2. "American Students Abroad Can't Be 'Global Citizens,'" *Chronicle of Higher Education*, March 7, 2008, A34.

3. Fogel, "Capitalism & Democracy in 2040."

4. Chinese National Bureau of Statistics, www.stats.gov.cn/english/.

5. "Clipping the Dragon's Wings," *Economist*, December 22, 2007; "The Numbers Game," *Newsweek*, January 31, 2000.

6. Fareed Zakaria, "The Rise of the Rest," *Newsweek*, May 3, 2008.

7. Zakaria, "The Rise of the Rest."

8. Accenture, "The Rise of the Multi-Polar World," 2007.

9. Ibid., 3.

10. As quoted in NASSCOM's Education Initiatives, "2007 Factsheet."

11. Claire Cozens, "Those Gaffes in Full," *MediaGuardian*, November 17, 2003.

12. Julie Jargon, "Kraft Reformulates Oreo, Scores in China," *Wall Street Journal*, May 1, 2008.

13. Mark Steyn, *America Alone: The End of the World as We Know It* (Washington, DC: Regnery, 2008), 173.

14. Gurcharan Das, *India Unbound* (New York: Knopf, 2001) and *The Elephant Paradigm: India Wrestles with Change* (New Delhi, India: Penguin Books India, 2002).

15. As quoted in Shailaja Neelakantan, "The Capitalist Case for India," *Asia Times*, March 8, 2003.

16. Gitanjali Prasad, *The Great Indian Family: New Roles, Old Responsibilities* (New York: Penguin Books, 2006).

17. As quoted from an interview with Gitanjali Prasad, "Will the Great Indian Family Survive?" www.rediff.com/news/2006/jul/05inter1 .htm?q=tp/.

18. Amol Sharma, Jackie Range, and Vibhuti Agarwal, "Outsourcing? Think Family," *Wall Street Journal*, May 27, 2008.

19. See the International Fund for Agricultural Development web site, www.ifad.org/events/remittances/maps/.

20. "Send Me a Number," *Economist*, January 3, 2008.

21. Author interview with Bashir Mohamed, May 13, 2008.

22. Author interview with Gurcharan Das, April 22, 2008, Mumbai, India.

23. Edward Luce, *In Spite of the Gods: The Rise of Modern India* (New York: Doubleday, 2007), 276.

24. Ibid., 257, 272–277.

25. Ibid., 276.

26. James McGregor, *One Billion Customers: Lessons from the Front Lines of Doing Business in China* (New York: Free Press, 2007), 233.

27. BBC News, "Three Gorges Dam Wall Completed," May 20, 2006.

28. David Lague, "1977 Exam Opened Escape Route into China's Elite," *New York Times*, January 6, 2008.

29. Accenture, "The Rise of the Multi-Polar World," 26.

30. Central Intelligence Agency, *World Factbook*, www.cia.gov/ library/publications/the-world-factbook/.

31. Gerald W. Bracey, "Heard the One about the 600,000 Chinese Engineers?" *Washington Post*, May 21, 2006.

32. McGregor, *One Billion Customers*, 262.

33. Ibid., 270.

34. To learn more about public-private partnerships, see the Government of India's Ministry of Finance web site, www.pppinindia .com.

Chapter 5: Winning the Battle for Talent

1. Accenture, "The Rise of the Multi-Polar World," 2007, 9.

2. Rainer Strack, Jens Baier, and Anders Fahlander, "Managing Demographic Risk," *Harvard Business Review*, February 2008.

3. "China Prepares for Fourth Baby Boom," May 5, 2006, CHINAdailycom.cn.

4. Tamara Erickson, *Retire Retirement: Career Strategies for the Boomer Generation* (Watertown, MA: Harvard School Business Press, 2008), 12.

5. Stephanie Armour, "Generation Y: They've Arrived at Work with a New Attitude," *USA Today*, November 5, 2005.

6. Carol Hymnowitz, "Marketers Focus More on Global 'Tribes' than on Nationalities," *Wall Street Journal*, December 10, 2007.

7. Accenture, "Rise of the Multi-Polar World."

8. "Review of National Action Plans on Youth Employment," *United Nations*, 2007, www.un.org/esa/socdev/poverty/documents/National.Action.Plans.2007.pdf.

9. *Wikipedia*, s.v. "generation gap," http://en.wikipedia.org/wiki/Generation_gap/.

10. Shannon Bond, OnPhilanthropy.com, "Recruiting Gen Y: The Importance of Corporate Social Engagement in Attracting Top Young Talent," October 10, 2007.

11. "Today's Leaders Are the Global Generation," *Management Issues*, February 22, 2008, www.management-issues.com/2008/2/21/research/todays-leaders-are-the-global-generation.asp.

12. Gregory Berns, *Satisfaction: The Science of Finding True Fulfillment* (New York: Henry Holt & Company, 2005).

13. Sarah Perez, "Why Gen Y Is Going to Change the Web," May 15, 2008, ReadWriteWeb.com.

14. A blog is a frequent, chronological publication of personal thoughts and web links. A person will use a blog to share opinions or post information that may be of interest to a subgroup or a general community. A wiki is a server program that allows users to collaborate in forming the content of a web site. File sharing is when one computer file can be accessed and updated by more than one user, through a network.

15. Forrester Research, "The State of Consumers and Technology: Benchmark 2006," August 1, 2006.

16. "Survey Shows Young Asians Fit 38 Hours of Activities into One Day (But Still Manage Eight Hours Sleep!)," *Synovate*, March 12, 2008.

17. Jon Swartz, "Social-Networking Sites Going Global," *USA Today*, February 2008.

18. "The Global Race among Social Networks Heats Up," February 27, 2008, TechCrunch.com.

19. Heather Havenstein, "Social Networking Quickly Taking Global Hold," *Computerworld*, August 1, 2007.

20. Gina Ruiz, "Job Boards Tap Facebook for Gen Y Workers," October 2, 2007, Workforce.com.

21. Ruiz, "Job Boards Tap Facebook for Gen Y Workers."

22. Perez, "Why Gen Y Is Going to Change the Web."

23. Taly Weiss, "Social Media Still on Rise: Comparative Global Study," *TrendSpotting.com*, April 23, 2008.

24. Perez, "Why Gen Y Is Going to Change the Web."

25. Gerrit Visser, "Social Networking and Web Access Part of Peoples Work Lives," June 23, 2007, SmartMobs.com.

26. For further reading, see Dion Hinchcliffe's blog, http://blogs.zdnet.com/Hinchcliffe/?p=150/.

27. The SMP web site was jointly developed by the Australian-based web agency C2 and the U.K.-based media consultancy, Elemental.

28. Norimitsu Onishi, "Broken Hearts, Sore Thumbs: Japan's Best Sellers Go Cellular," *New York Times*, January 20, 2008.

29. Lee Gomes, "U.S. Gets Prepared for Digital Television," *Wall Street Journal*, January 22, 2008.

30. Julia Flynn, "Virtual Expats Work Abroad without Leaving Home," *Wall Street Journal*, October 19, 1999.

31. Shannon Bond, "Recruiting Gen Y: The Importance of Corporate Social Engagement in Attracting Top Young Talent," October 10, 2007, OnPhilanthropy.com.

32. David Wigder, Senior Vice President, Strategy and Analysis of Digitas (a Publicis company) and contributor to the consortium Future Lab Marketing and Innovation, "Going Green to Recruit and Retain Employees," October 1, 2007.

33. Jim Pickard and Fiona Harvey, "The Wilting Agenda: Britain Loses Its Appetite for Green Initiatives," *Financial Times*, May 28, 2008.

34. Nicholas D. Kristof, "The Age of Ambition," *New York Times*, January 27, 2008.

35. Daina Lawrence, "Youngsters Take the Helm to Combat Child Sex Trade," *Financial Times*, January 25, 2008.

36. George Cole, "A Catalyst for Change," *Financial Times*, January 25, 2008.

37. Nicholas D. Kristof, "The Age of Ambition," *New York Times*, January 27, 2008.

Chapter 6: Women Working

1. Donald Morrison, "Women Hold Up Half the Sky," *Time*, February 14, 2005.

2. International Labor Office, "Global Employment Trends for Women," March 1, 2008, www.ilo.org/public/english/employment/strat/download/getw08.pdf.

3. See the World Bank web site for GenderStats database of gender statistics, http://devdata.worldbank.org/genderstats/.

4. Sheli Z. Rosenberg, "Why Aren't There More Women on Boards?" *Directorship*, April–May 2008, 55.

5. "Enter the Dragons," *Chief Executive Officer*, September 2007.

6. "The Entrepreneurship GenderGap in Global Perspective: Implications for Effective Policymaking to Support Female Entrepreneurship," briefing note no. 22, *CGO Insights*, October 2005.

7. International Labor Office, "Global Employment Trends for Women."

8. Ibid., 2.

9. "Women Hold Up Half the Sky," *Global Economics Weekly*, March 5, 2008, 3; https://portal.gs.com.

10. "Women & Decision Making: Meeting Challenges," International Women's Day, March 8, 2006.

11. For more information, see the prefecture's web site, www.pref.fukuoka.lg.jp/somu/multilingual/english/top.html.

12. Karin Klenke, *Women and Leadership*, (New York: Springer Publishing, 1996), 2.

13. Ibid., 3.

14. Ibid., 4.

15. "Women Hold Up Half the Sky," Goldman Sachs Global Economics paper no. 164, March 5, 2008.

16. UNESCO.org, EFA Global Monitoring Report 2008, http://portal.unesco.org/education/en/cv.php-URL_ID=49591&URL_DO=DO_TOPIC&URL_SECTION=201.

17. "Less than Half of Female Professionals Feel Prepared to Succeed in Global Business Environment of 2011," *Accenture*, March 6, 2008.

18. "A Beloved Professor Delivers the Lecture of a Lifetime," *Wall Street Journal*, September 15, 2007.

19. The image of Rosie the Riveter was drawn by Norman Rockwell, who based his work on Rose Will Monroe, a native Texan who moved to Michigan to build bombers for the U.S. Air Force. Ms. Monroe was also featured in a promotional film called *Rosie the Riveter*. A picture commissioned by Westinghouse in 1942 by J. Howard Miller, which features a woman with a red bandanna and raised fist under the caption "We Can Do It!" is often mistaken for an image of Rosie. For further reading, see Sherna Berger Gluck, *Rosie the Riveter Revisited: Women, the War, and Social Change* (New York: Plume, 1988); Matilda Butler and Kendra Bonnett, *Rosie's Daughters: The "First Woman To" Generation Tells Its Story* (Berkeley, CA: Iaso Books, 2007).

20. Betty Friedan, *The Feminine Mystique* (New York: Dell, 1964).

21. 1996 national opinion poll published by the Center for Policy Alternatives.

22. International Labor Office, "Global Employment Trends for Women," 2.

23. Jason Karaian, "Chosen Few," *CFO Europe*, March 2007, 29.

24. Greg Burns, "Nobody's Business but Her Own," *Chicago Tribune Magazine*, October 14, 2007, 14–17.

25. Alex Kuczynski, "Ruth Whitney, 71, the Editor Who Made Glamour Relevant," *New York Times*, June 5, 1999.

26. Karen Hughes remarks at the Hawaii Governor's Conference, August 29, 2006.

27. Karaian, "Chosen Few," 28.

28. Ibid., 30.

29. Author interview with Deb Morrin, June 23, 2008.

30. Accenture, "One Step Ahead of 2011: A New Horizon for Working Women," 6.

31. Nancy J. Adler, "Leading beyond Boundaries," in *Enlightened Power: How Women Are Transforming the Practice of Leadership*, ed. Linda Coughlin, Ellen Wingard, Keith Hollihan (San Francisco, CA: Jossey-Bass, 2005), 351–366.

32. Ibid., 358.

33. Hughes remarks at the Hawaii Governor's Conference.

34. Ibid.

35. "Women and Entrepreneurship in Chile—2005/2006," *Global Entrepreneurship Monitor* (Babson College and the London Business School).

36. As quoted in Venkatesan Vembu, "How Am I Any Less?" *Daily News and Analysis India*, October 28, 2006.

37. Sharon Reier, "In Europe, Women Gain on Boards," *New York Times*, March 22, 2008, B4.

38. Karaian, "Chosen Few," 28.

39. Anne Fisher, "Readers Weigh In on Work and Women Abroad," *Fortune*, March 29, 1999, 200.

40. Adler, "Leading beyond Boundaries," 356.

41. Ibid., 362.

Chapter 7: Shareholder Interests

1. Geoffrey Jones, "Restoring a Global Economy, 1950–1980," *Harvard Business School's Working Knowledge*, August 22, 2005.

2. JETRO report on Japan-Mexico Economic Partnership agreement, www.jetro.go.jp/en/news/releases/20060407850-news/.

3. See the United Nations Conference on Trade and Development report on Development and Globalization, http://unctad.org/en/docs/gdscsir20071_en.pdf.

4. Accenture, "The Rise of the Emerging-Market Multinational," 2007, 2.

5. *Fortune* Global 500, 2007, money.cnn.com/magazines/fortune/global500/2007/full_list/.

6. "PetroChina World's 1st $1 Trillion Company," November 5, 2007, CBSNews.com.

7. *Wikipedia*, s.v., "Tata Group," http://en.wikipedia.org/wiki/Tata_Group/.

8. Author interview with Peter Drucker, August 7, 2001.

9. Bureau of Labor Statistics as quoted in "Sharp Decline in Union Members," *New York Times*, January 27, 2007.

10. "Trade: France Plans to Push for Extension of EU Farm Subsidies," IPS/GIN via Comtex news release Paris, March 24, 2008.

11. "Why the French Love Their Farmers," *International Herald Tribune*, December 1, 2005.

12. La Tribune, November 7, 2005, as quoted in www.oxfam.org/en/news/pressreleases2005/pr051107_france_eu/.

13. Roger Cohen, "New Day in the Americas," *New York Times*, January 6, 2008.

14. Neil King Jr. and Greg Hitt, "Dubai Ports World Sells U.S. Assets," *Wall Street Journal*, December 1, 2006.

15. Georg Szalai, "Hollywood Primes the Pump for Oil Money from the Mideast," *Hollywood Reporter*, December 7, 2007.

16. Blythe McGarvie, "Consumer Consumption or Socialized Capital," *Brunswick Group*, 2001.

17. "Hungry like the Wolf," *Economist*, May 8, 2008.

18. "Flying the Flag," *Economist*, May 15, 2008.

19. Aaron Bernstein, "How Cross-Border Government Investments Are Shaking Up Western Economies," *Directorship*, April–May 2008, 34.

20. Steven M. Davidoff, "A Guide to Speed Dating with Sovereign Funds," *New York Times*, January 15, 2008.

21. "The Rise of the Emerging-Market Multinational," *Accenture*, 2007, 22.

22. Bernstein, "How Cross-Border Government Investments Are Shaking Up Western Economies."

23. Accenture, "The Rise of the Emerging-Market Multinational," 22.

24. Peter Weinberg, "Sovereign Funds Offer a Wealth of Benefits," *Financial Times*, May 23, 2008.

25. Weinberg, "Sovereign Funds Offer a Wealth of Benefits."

26. Peter Goodman and Louise Story, "Foreign Investors Buy U.S.

Holdings at a Record Pace," *International Herald Tribune*, January 20, 2008.

27. "Silence of the Sage," March 4, 2008, Economist.com.

28. "A Guide to Speed Dating with Sovereign Funds."

29. Weinberg, "Sovereign Funds Offer a Wealth of Benefits."

30. Chip Cummins, "Abu Dhabi Sets Investment Code," *Wall Street Journal*, March 19, 2008.

31. Yousef al Otaiba, "Our Sovereign Wealth Plans," *Wall Street Journal*, March 19, 2008.

32. Accenture, Economist Intelligence Unit ViewsWire, "Join the Club," May 1, 2008.

33. Bernstein, "How Cross-Border Government Investments Are Shaking Up Western Economies," 33.

34. Ibid., 34.

35. John Bogle, *The Soul of Capitalism* (New Haven, CT: Yale University Press, 2005), 128.

36. Ibid., xix.

37. Ibid., 43.

38. *The Viking Network*, s.v. "legendary Viking," www.viking.no/e/people/e-knud.htm.

39. Martin Wolf, "Preserving the Open Economy at Times of Stress," May 20, 2008, FT.com.

Chapter 8: Entrepreneurs from A to Z

1. John A. Byrne, "The Man Who Invented Management," *BusinessWeek*, November 28, 2005.

2. Celia Dugger, "Ending Famine, Simply by Ignoring the Experts," *New York Times*, December 2, 2007.

3. *Dictionary.com*, "entrepreneur," http://dictionary.reference.com/browse/entrepreneur.

4. John Willman, "Single-Minded about Changing the Market System," *Financial Times*, January 14, 2008.

5. *Wikipedia*, s.v. "entrepreneur," http://en.wikipedia.org/wiki/Entrepreneur/.

6. A.G. Lafley and Ram Charan, *The Game-Changer: How You Can Drive Revenue and Profit Growth with Innovation* (New York: Crown Business, 2008, 243).

7. Charles Handy, *The Elephant and the Flea* (Watertown, MA: Harvard Business School Press, 2003), 147.

8. Adam Smith, *The Theory of Moral Sentiments* (Indianapolis, IN: Liberty Classics, 1976), 184–185.

9. "New Rules for a Globalized World," *Aspen Idea*, Summer 2005.

10. A.G. Lafley and Ram Charan, *The Game Changer* (New York: Crown Business, 2008), 269–271.

11. See German language version, Rolf-Christian Wentz, *The Innovation Machine* (New York: Springer, 2007); see also www.the-innovation-machine.com for English excerpts.

12. Satish Nambisan and Mohanbir Sawhney, *The Global Brain* (Upper Saddle River, NJ: Wharton School Publishing, 2008).

13. Richard Florida, *The Flight of the Creative Class: The New Global Competition for Talent* (New York: HarperCollins, 2005), 143.

14. See the Haier company web site, www.haier.com/AboutHaier/HaierWorldwide/.

15. John Feffer, "The Big Yam," *Nation*, January 31, 2008.

16. Paul Boutin, "Are the Browser Wars Back?" June 30, 2004, Slate.com.

17. Dawn C. Chmielewski, "DVD Format War Appears to Be Over," *Los Angeles Times*, January 5, 2008.

18. Michael E. Porter, *Competitive Strategy*, (New York: Free Press, 1980), 4.

19. *Wikipedia*, s.v. "dabbawallas," http://en.wikipedia.org/wiki/Dabbawala; see also the *dabbawalla* web site, www.dabbawalla.com.

20. See www.dabbawalla.com.

21. Saritha Rai, "In India, Grandma Cooks, They Deliver," *New York Times*, May 29, 2008.

22. World Economic Forum, Global Competitiveness Report 2007–2008, www.weforum.org/en/initiatives/gcp/Global%20Competitiveness%20Report/index.htm.

23. Central Intelligence Agency, *The 2008 World Factbook*, for country profiles of both Denmark and Singapore, www.cia.gov.

24. John D. Gartner, *The Hypomanic Edge* (New York: Simon & Schuster, 2005), 2–3.

25. Ibid., 12.

26. Eve Tahmincioglu, "Moving Money, Not Telegrams, Across Borders," *New York Times*, June 7, 2008, B2.

27. Carlos M. Gutierrez and Arnold Schwarzenegger, "Keep America Open to Trade," *Wall Street Journal*, May 12, 2008.

28. "Come, Entrepreneurs!" *Asahi Shinbun*, June 29, 2002.

29. Yuka Hayashi, "Japan Taps Foreign Nurses in Labor Squeeze," *Wall Street Journal*, May 23, 2008.

30. Nicholas Bavarez, "No Capitalism, Please, We're French," *Financial Times*, December 2, 1999.

31. John Tagliabue, "Pace of Change Too Slow to Keep Entrepreneurs in France," *New York Times*, March 11, 2008.

32. www.mckinseyquarterly.com/How_companies_act_on_global_trends_A_McKinsey_Global_Survey_2130/.

33. Donald N. Sull, "Why Good Companies Go Bad," *Harvard Business Review*, July–August 1999.

Chapter 9: Values and Global Context

1. Mark D. McGarvie, *One Nation Under Law: America's Early National Struggles to Separate Church and State* (Dekalb: Northern Illinois Press, 2004), 68.

2. Mark D. McGarvie, Ph.D., unpublished essay, 2008, University of Richmond, VA, School of Arts & Sciences, Prelaw Advisor and Lecturer in History and Leadership Studies.

3. Nathan Sharansky, "Democracies Can't Compromise on Core Values," *Wall Street Journal*, June 16, 2008, A15.

4. Gary P. Ferraro, *The Cultural Dimension of International Business* (Upper Saddle River, NJ: Prentice Hall, 2005), 97.

5. Martin Fackler, "The Japanese Salaryman Is Starting to Blow the Whistle," *New York Times*, June 7, 2008.

6. Ferraro, *The Cultural Dimension of International Business*, 109.

7. Gregory L. White and Guy Chazan, "Boardroom Brawl Roils BP's Russia Venture," *Wall Street Journal*, June 12, 2008.

8. David Jolly, "Russia Bars Chief of Joint Venture, BP Says," *New York Times*, August 14, 2008.

9. See CNN.com special on the origins of the Cold War, www.cnn.com/SPECIALS/cold.war/episodes/14/documents/debate/.

10. Mark Hornung, Bernard Hodes Group, "The Case for Employer Branding," www.hodes.com/publications/interviews/hornung.asp.

11. Peter Cheese, Robert J. Thomas, and Elizabeth Craig, *The Talent Powered Organization: Strategies for Globalization, Talent Management, and High Performance* (London: Kogan Page, 2007).

12. Interview with author, June 10, 2008.

13. Ibid.

14. See Tesco case study, www.employerbrand.com.

15. See the Johnson & Johnson web site for company credo, www.jnj.com/connect/about-jnj/jnj-credo/.

16. Henry B. Veatch, *Rational Man: A Modern Interpretation of Aristotelian Ethics* (Bloomington: Indiana University Press, 1962), 91.

17. Laura Nash and Howard Stevenson, *Just Enough: Tools for Creating Success in Your Work and Life* (Hoboken, NJ: John Wiley & Sons, 2004).

Epilogue: Continuing Your Journey to New Horizons

1. Sridhar Pappu, "Angry White Man," *Mother Jones*, January 2007.

2. Ibid.

Index